TRUMPED
AN ALTERNATIVE MUSICAL

This edition first published in 2020 by Blue Lens
Blue Lens is an imprint of Blue Lens Films Limited

Blue Lens Films Limited, 71-75 Shelton Street,
Covent Garden, London, WC2H 9JQ, United Kingdom

ISBN 978 1 913408 79 4
1 3 5 9 10 8 6 4 2

Printer and binder may vary between territories of
production and sale

LICENSE INFORMATION

Subject to the terms and conditions set out in this book, the purchase* of this book entitles you to be granted a one-time non-transferable performance license for the material with the following conditions:

VERSION	TRUMPED: An Alternative Musical, Act II
LICENSE TYPE	Amateur Two Performance *See terms for eligibility criteria*
LICENSE AREA	Australia, Canada, European Economic Area, New Zealand, South Africa, United Kingdom, United States
NUMBER OF PERFORMANCES	Maximum of two performances
MAXIMUM AUDIENCE	Not to exceed 300 in aggregate
TICKET PRICE RESTRICTIONS	Not to exceed USD 10.00 (or foreign equivalent) per ticket, or USD 1,800 (or foreign equivalent) in aggregate.

*Only the first purchaser of this book is entitled to be granted a performance license. Used or resold copies do not entitle you to a performance license.

To register for your license, please complete the online for at analternativemusical.com/performancelicenses.

TERMS OF LICENSE

1) Subject to these terms, the first purchaser of this book ("the licensee") (defined as the individual/ organization to first purchase this copy from a recognized registered book retailer), is entitled to be granted by Toupee or Not Toupee Limited (a UK based company managing the rights to TRUMPED: An Alternative Musical on behalf of the rights holders), a one-time non-transferable performance or use license for the material contained within this book.

2) No performance license will be granted for purchasers of used or resold copies of this book.

3) No performance or performance-related work may begin until a performance license has been granted to the licensee.

4) The granting of a performance license is subject to the successful registration of the licensee and their purchase of this book. Satisfactory proof of first purchase is required before a license is granted.

5) Licensees can register their book purchase at analternativemusical.com/performancelicenses.

6) The license must register before January 1, 2022. No license will be granted for registrations after this date. All licenses (except educational use) will be valid for a period of twelve months. Any and all performance-related work and performances must take place within this period. Educational use licenses will be valid for a period of three months. Any use, performance-related work or performances undertaken outside of this period will be deemed unlicensed use.

7) Licenses will be granted subject to the terms and with the conditions as set out within this book. License terms or conditions will not be varied under any circumstance.

8) Only one license will be granted per book and each licensee is limited to a maximum of five licenses.

9) Educational licenses are available only to registered non-profit educational organizations within the license area.

10) Non-profit licenses are available only to registered non-profit organizations within the license area.

11) Amateur licensees are available only to amateur performance groups within the license area and with annual revenues not exceeding USD 25,000 (or foreign equivalent) in the previous financial year.

12) Licenses are valid only within the license area, defined as: The United States, United Kingdom, European Economic Area, Canada, Australia, New Zealand, and South Africa.

13) Once a purchase is registered, a license cannot be canceled for any reason.

14) Once a license is granted, the licensee is required to enter the license number on each page of this book in the designated area, after which, copies of the material may be made in order to distribute for performance or education use as the license allows. No copying is permitted without a license number being entered on each page. Licensees are required to control and note the number of copies of the material being made. All copies must be returned to the licensee and destroyed at the end of the material's licensed use.

15) Once licensed, subject to the conditions of that license and these terms, the licensee is permitted to produce the material contained within this book for public performance. This does not apply to educational use licenses which grant the license to use the material in a purely educational environment with performances permitted to non-paying audiences not exceeding 30 persons.

16) Licensees must produce the material in full with no edits of any kind (substitutions, additions or subtractions) permitted. In the circumstance of extract licenses, the licensee is permitted to choose up to fifteen scenes to produced. These scenes must be produced in full with no edits of any kind (substitutions, additions or subtractions) permitted.

17) Performances must take place at a premises which is owned and/or controlled by the licensee. No performances may take place as part of a festival in any territory or within 50 miles of a city where a current arts festival is taking place during that festival.

18) No additional rights, including, but not limited to, artwork, likeness, trademarks (registered or otherwise), or any other intellectual property is included as part of any license. No license is granted for any music, tune, incidental music, or any other material which may, in some circumstances, be held by third party rights holders.

19) Licensees are required to observe all relevant local, state, and national laws, and any relevant union agreement. Under no circumstances will the retailer, distributor, publisher, Toupee or Not Toupee Limited, the

rights holders, or any other third party be liable to the licensee or any person, group, or organization associated with the licensee, for any loss or liability which the licensee experiences or which is incurred as a result of a license being granted.

20) In no circumstance will the livability of the retailer, distributor, publisher, Toupee or Not Toupee Limited, the rights holders, or any other third party be liable to the licensee or any person, group, or organization associated with the licensee, exceed the United States list price of this book at the time of purchase.

21) For performances taking place in the United Kingdom or the European Economic Area, the licensee may be required to pay VAT in addition to the purchase of this book. No performance license will be granted until this is paid.

22) The licensee and any person, group, or organization associated with the licensee, must not bring the the retailer, distributor, publisher, Toupee or Not Toupee Limited, the rights holders, or any other third party into disrepute. This includes, but is not limited to, by sharing hateful messages and/or content, and using the licensed material in any way except that explicitly permitted in their license. Should Toupee or Not Toupee Limited decide that the licensee or any person, group, or organization associated with the licensee has breached this term, the license granted will be revoked without compensation to the licensee.

23) The licensee must ensure that they do not associate themselves or lead any person to believe they are associated with the retailer, distributor, publisher, Toupee or Not Toupee Limited, the rights holders, or any other third party.

24) Should the purchaser of this book be ineligible for a license, no refund of this book will be given. Should the licensee breach any term or condition of the license, the license granted will be revoked without compensation to the licensee.

INTRODUCTION

Written in four acts presented across two parts, TRUMPED: An Alternative Musical is a satirical stage play that parodies the 2016 Presidential Election campaign of Donald Trump and his subsequent time in office as the 45th President of the United States.

Opening on the final day of the July 2016 Republican National Convention in Cleveland, Ohio, Act I tells the story behind the Trump campaign's journey from the outsider of the Republican field to the unexpected winner of the Electoral College with a questionable victory.

Covering the Russia meeting at Trump Tower, all three election debates against the Democratic opponent, Hillary Clinton, and the attempts of the Russian President, Vladimir Putin, to ensure a win for the Trump campaign in the state of Wisconsin, Act I concludes at the end of November 8, election day, as the final results come in.

With the election over and Donald Trump set to become the 4th President, Act II opens the day following the election as both the world and the current President, Barack Obama, are all still in shock at the previous day's result.

Concluding toward the end of Trump's first year in office, Act II covers his and his Vice President, Mike Pence's inaugurations, a visit to the White House by his German counterpart, Angela Merkel, and the apparent early collapse of the Trump regime brought about through the actions of Robert Mueller, the tweets of Donald Trump Junior, and the gullibility of Eric Trump, forcing the family to make a quick escape and leave another to fall in their place as Part One comes to a close.

Picking up some weeks after the conclusion of Part One, Act III opens as the President is presumed missing by his closet supporters, and Vladimir Putin is becoming tiresome of ruling from the front lines.

With the job of bringing Trump back to the United States tasked to him, Fox News anchor, Sean Hannity, soon sets off to South America to discover that his journey home is to

(CONTINUED)

CONTINUED:

be hindered by the measures he supported.

Coming to a close as the 2018 Midterm elections approach,
Act III follows the President as, despite his America-first
attitude, he attempts to forge new international ties with
world leaders and royalty alike, while domestically, his
party works to secure a new seat on the Supreme Court.

Act IV opens with an opportunity to discover how Trump's
predecessor is coping with his post-presidential life and
his thoughts on the upcoming Midterm elections. Leaving
island life behind, the action then returns to Trump as he
discovers that under his leadership, the Republican Party
is set for a historic loss.

Following the Midterms being brought to you live from
Florida and Texas, Act IV goes on to tell the story of a
government shutdown and fine dining Trump-style as the
Democrats begin searching for their 2020 nominee.

Coming to a close in late 2019, this final act builds up to
an interpretation of events as they should have been, with
the President finally being held to account.

CAST OF CHARACTERS

All characters are listed in order of appearance.

THE NARRATOR, Narrator of TRUMPED: An Alternative Musical
HILLARY CLINTON, Presidential Candidate/ Former Sec. State
DONALD TRUMP, Presidential Candidate/ 45th President
VLADIMIR PUTIN, President of Russia/ American Supreme Ruler
PRESS #1, CNN Journalist
PRESS #2, New York Times Journalist
PRESS #3, Washington Post Journalist
PRESS #4, NBC Journalist
PRESS #5, Fox News Journalist
PRESS #6, MSNBC Journalist
BARACK OBAMA, 44th President
KELLYANNE CONWAY, Campaign Manager to Donald Trump
CHRIS CHRISTIE, Governor of New Jersey
BILL CLINTON, 42nd President/ Husband to Hillary Clinton
DONALD TRUMP JR, Son to Donald Trump
IVANKA TRUMP, Daughter to Donald Trump
ERIC TRUMP, Son to Donald Trump/ Eric
SEAN SPICER, White House Press Secretary
MICHELLE OBAMA, First Lady
MIKE PENCE, Running Mate to Donald Trump/ Vice-President
ANGELA MERKEL, Chancellor of Germany
ANDERSON COOPER, CNN News Anchor/ Second Debate Moderator
PAUL RYAN, Speaker of the House
PRODUCTION ASSISTANT, Assistant to Anderson Cooper
JARED KUSHNER, Son-in-Law and Advisor to Donald Trump
DAY CARE ASSISTANT, White House Day Care Assistant
ANTHONY SCARAMUCCI, Director of Communications
SARAH HUCKABEE SANDERS, White House Press Secretary
DELIVERY MAN #1, White House Delivery Worker
DELIVERY MAN #2, White House Delivery Worker
ROBERT MUELLER, Former FBI Director/ Special Counsel
RUDY GIULIANI, Former NYC Mayor/ Lawyer to Donald Trump
FBI AGENT #1, Agent for the FBI
FBI AGENT #2, Agent for the FBI
CHECK-IN AGENT, Airport Check-In Agent
SEAN HANNITY, Fox News Anchor

PRODUCTION NOTES

At all performances, the production crew should ensure that a message is played to audiences in order to inform them that while based upon and satirizing true events, TRUMPED: An Alternative Musical, Part One and Two, should not be considered a true or accurate record or representation of those events, nor should it be considered to portray the individuals satirized within accurately.

At all performances, a seat should be resaved at the end of the row within the audience for the character of Hillary Clinton to make her entrance from in Act I, Scene 7. This seat should be within the front orchestra section and be viewable, as far as reasonably possible, by all sections of the auditorium.

To cover the high number of characters within TRUMPED: An Alternative Musical, the majority of company members should perform multiple roles. This excludes the company member who is playing the role of the Narrator.

Where the script refers to the Ensemble, this should be taken to mean all company members, who are available at the time of that scene (i.e., not performing a different role within the scene or undertaking a wardrobe change), except for where specific exemptions are noted within the script.

The note that follows the introduction of the ensemble provides additional information on the role which the ensemble is performing in that scene (e.g., "ENSEMBLE (as PRESS").

In some instances, specific characters will be included as part of the ensemble (e.g., "Press #1").

At no point should company members performing the role of the Narrator or Donald Trump be included within the ensemble.

Performances of TRUMPED: An Alternative Musical should not require additional ensemble members outside of principal company members and understudies.

(CONTINUED)

CONTINUED:

The role of the Narrator is nonspecific for casting
purposes, and freedom should be offered to this company
member to perform their own style of narration (within the
direction of the written material and director).

With the majority of characters in TRUMPED: An Alternative
Musical based upon real people and to be performed as
impersonations and parodies, company members should be
given the freedom (within the direction of the written
material and director) to perform the impersonation as they
feel most appropriate. This may include the changing of
minor words, the mispronunciation of words and phrases, or
varying the pace of delivery.

"Cardboard Melania" should be achieved through the creation
of a life-size cardboard cutout of Melania Trump being
attached to an RC vehicle, which is controlled from
offstage.

<u>Dialogue</u>   Indicates that dialogue should be
                mispronounced.

Dialogue   Indicates that dialogue should be
                emphasized.

/DIALOGUE/   Indicates that dialogue should be sung.

PART ONE

ACT II : "THE FIRST YEAR"

ACT II, SCENE ONE | ACT II OPENING

> With the audience seated once
> again, the lights across the
> auditorium go down, and the
> anticipation is allowed to build
> on the empty stage before a
> single spotlight shines, and the
> music begins.

NARRATOR
(entering)
/YOU MIGHT BE THINKING YOU'RE IN THR WRONG SHOW, BUT NO
NEED TO WORRY, FOR THIS IS JUST A PARODY SONG, WHICH JUST
LIKE THIS PARODY PRESIDENT SHOULDN'T LAST LONG.

A TREASONOUS RACIST, MISOGYNIST, ALL TOGETHER HATED MAN IN
THE WHITE HOUSE, WHAT - THE - HELL'S - HE - TWEETED - NOW?/

> A light goes up on CLINTON, who
> stands drinking from a bottle of
> wine.

CLINTON
/CAN WE ALL SCREAM NOW?/

NARRATOR
(gesturing at the bottle)
Please?

> The NARRATOR takes the bottle,
> drinks from it, and then hands
> it back before she exits.

NARRATOR
/YOU CAN'T BELIEVE IT YET, YOU HAVEN'T HAD THE CHANCE, HIS
WHOLE VOTER BASE IS CLEARLY IN A TRANCE, AND SOMEHOW HE
CAN'T EVEN FIND TO WEAR, CORRECTLY - FITTING - PANTS./

(CONTINUED)

                              The stage fills with light as
                              the ENSEMBLE stand in a line. In
                              front of them, TRUMP, his pants
                              clearly too tight.

                         ENSEMBLE
/DONALD TRUMP IS AN ORANGE MAN (WITH VERY TINY HANDS), AND
HE HAS RACIST FANS --/

                          TRUMP
WAIT!

                              The music stops, and the
                              ENSEMBLE clear the stage.

                          TRUMP
I do not like this song. This song is from a show I do not
like, which I hear is highly overrated and also not so
great. The cast was also very mean to Mike Pence, and Mike
Pence deserves better. He has had a very tough life
because, for the last fifty-seven years, he has had to live
as Mike Pence.

                         NARRATOR
Mister President-Elect --

                          TRUMP
No one, except the audience of this show perhaps, has ever
had a tougher time in a theater than Mike Pence. Especially
no politician.

                         NARRATOR
What about President Abraham Lincoln?

                              Beat.

                         CLINTON
                     (leaning on stage)
I just want to say, I like that show. I'm down with that
relatable stuff. I love rap, it's what Bill and I order as
a sandwich when we feel adventurous.

                          TRUMP
Go away, Crooked Hillary Clinton.

                                             (CONTINUED)

PERFORMANCE LICENSE EDITION   LICENSE # _ _ _ _ _ _ _ _

                    CLINTON exits.

                         TRUMP
Can we sing something different?

                         NARRATOR
Sure, I've got another.

                         The NARRATOR stamps their foot.

                         The music begins, and the
                         ENSEMBLE enters wearing TRUMP
                         masks.

                         ENSEMBLE
/TRUMPY LUMPY TRUMPETY DOO, HE...
                    (pointing at TRUMP)
DOESN'T GIVE A DAMN ABOUT YOU.
                    (pointing at the audience)
TRUMPY LUMPY TRUMPETY DEE.../

                         Stepping forward and removing
                         their mask, one of the ENSEMBLE
                         reveal themselves as PUTIN.

                         PUTIN
                    (bringing a tape from his
                    pocket)
/I HAVE TAPE WHERE HE BE COVERED IN PEE./

                         The music stops, and the
                         ENSEMBLE clear to leave the
                         NARRATOR, PUTIN, and TRUMP.

                         TRUMP
What tape?

                         PUTIN
Well, Donald, that tape.

                         TRUMP
But you cannot have that tape. It does not exist.

                                        (CONTINUED)

                          PUTIN
                   (holding the tape up)
It exist. I have tape here. It show you covered in pee-pee.

                          TRUMP
I do not remember that happening.

                          PUTIN
Really, do you not? What about in Moscow?

                          TRUMP
I do not remember being in Moscow.

                          PUTIN
In Ritz Carlton hotel?

                          TRUMP
I do not remember staying at the Ritz Carlton hotel.

                          PUTIN
In presidential suite?

                          TRUMP
I do not remember staying in the presidential suite.

                          PUTIN
Their names be Dominika and Kristina.

                          Beat.

                          TRUMP
I remember.
                   (moving closer)
Do you have the bit where?

                          PUTIN
Yes.

                          TRUMP
What about the bit where they --

                          PUTIN
Yes.

                                                    (CONTINUED)

                              TRUMP
How about the bit where --

                              PUTIN
I have all of it, Donald.

                              TRUMP
Even the bit where...

                                        TRUMP whispers into PUTIN'S ear,
                                        and PUTIN's expression turns to
                                        one of disgust.

                              PUTIN
No. I not know you did that.
                         (beat)
You are it after?

                                        PUTIN notices the NARRATOR stood
                                        watching them.

                              PUTIN
Hello, Narrator. May I ask you, would you care to see
people you know ever again?

                              NARRATOR
Yes, I would.

                              PUTIN
Then listen to me. You need to help out old Uncle Putin, do
you understand?

                              NARRATOR
Yes.

                              PUTIN
Good, then I need you, as I believe you put it in west...
go away and tell no one about what you just heard. Do you
still understand me?

                              NARRATOR
I think so.

                                                            (CONTINUED)

                         PUTIN
Good. Then go away.

                    The NARRATOR exits.

                         PUTIN
Now then, Donald.

                         TRUMP
Yes, Comrade Vladimir Putin, sir.

                         PUTIN
We need to talk.

                         TRUMP
Are you breaking up with America?

                         PUTIN
No. Why would I break up with America? It take big effort
to rig election?
                         (beat)
But there be things that I need to make sure you understand
now that you be President of United States.

                         TRUMP
Yes, Comrade, sir.

                         PUTIN
Number one. You belong to Putin.

                         Beat.

                         TRUMP
What is number two?

                         PUTIN
There be no number two. Putin not want to confuse you with
big numbers.

                         TRUMP
Thank you, Comrade Vladimir Putin, sir.

                                              (CONTINUED)

                              PUTIN
I own you now, Donald. You do Putin say when Putin tell
you. Do you understand me?

                              TRUMP
Yes, sir.

                              PUTIN
And should you fail to obey, this tape of golden moment of
become public.

                              TRUMP
I will do whatever you say.

                              PUTIN
Very good. I see message has gotten across. Kneel.

                              TRUMP
What?

                              PUTIN
I said kneel.

                    TRUMP kneels before him.

                              PUTIN
Now crawl offstage.

                    TRUMP does as he's told.

                              PUTIN
                         (to audience)
I know where all of you live also.

                    PUTIN exits.

ACT II, SCENE TWO | TRUMP MEETS WITH OBAMA

                         At first, a dark and empty
                         stage.

                                        (CONTINUED)

                         NARRATOR
                      (entering)
Well, I think we can all agree that got weird.
                      (beat)
And so it is that with the election over, the world sits in
shock, for America has elected to get a new president who
all expect to run amok. But before we can reach the day of
his inauguration, a day which many feel can never come too
late, the new President-Elect is off to meet with the man
who previously, he had feelings toward of nothing but hate.

                              As the NARRATOR exits, lights go
                              up on the OVAL OFFICE, where the
                              ENSEMBLE (as PRESS) sit in front
                              of TRUMP, who himself is sat
                              waiting next to an empty chair.

                         TRUMP
Do any of you know where he is? I thought he would be here
by now. He said he would be here ten minutes ago. I know
some people would call this late. I would never say that,
but some people would. I guess we do have to let him off,
right? He does have a long commute. Did you know that the
guy flies in from Kenya every morning?

                              A spotlight finds OBAMA at the
                              other side of the stage drinking
                              shots. After a moment, he slaps
                              himself on the face and then
                              walks over to TRUMP.

                         TRUMP
                      (standing)
Oh, here is he. He has made it. Mister President, it is
good to see you.

                         OBAMA
Oh... my... god...

                              They both sit.

                         PRESS #1
Mister President, Mister President-Elect, how are you both
feeling about last night's result?

                                             (CONTINUED)

                    TRUMP
                 (to OBAMA)
Would you like to start?

                    OBAMA

Oh... my... god...

                    TRUMP

I guess I am starting then. Well, press journalist person,
I do not know your name --

                    PRESS #1
It's Rachel, I'm from C-N-N --

                    TRUMP

Fake news. You are fake news. I do not care about your
name, but I do care that I am very pleased about the result
last night. It was great, it could not have gone any more
great, it was just fantastic.

                         OBAMA lets out an audible groan.

                    TRUMP
                 (to OBAMA)
Would you like to say anything?

                    OBAMA

Oh... my... god...

                    TRUMP

I think we are ready for the next question.

                    PRESS #2
Mister President-Elect, you've made quite a few strongly-
worded statements over the years about the President, often
criticizing his judgments and actions. So will you be
calling on him for advice as you enter office yourself?

                    TRUMP

That is fake news. I have never said anything bad about
this man.

                    OBAMA

Oh... my... god...

                                          (CONTINUED)

CONTINUED:

                         PRESS #2
Mister Trump, that simply isn't true. In the past you have
spent years leading a moment questioning where the
President was born, you have accused him of being the
founder of ISIS, and you have said multiple times that you
feel he is the worse leader that America has ever had.

                         TRUMP
Correct. Fake news. Next question.

                         PRESS #3
President Obama, have you had the chance to speak to
Secretary Clinton this morning? Do you know if she's doing
okay?

                              A scream comes from somewhere
                              backstage.

                         OBAMA
Oh... my... god...

                         CLINTON (OFF)
Nearly three million votes. Three million.

                              OBAMA points towards the wings
                              and stands.

                         PRESS #4
Mister President, do you need to attend to that?

                              OBAMA begins to nod then slowly
                              begins shaking his head.

                         OBAMA
Oh... my... god...

                         PRESS #4
We understand, sir.

                              OBAMA exits.

                         TRUMP
Wait, where is he going? He is being very rude toward me.

PERFORMANCE LICENSE EDITION   LICENSE # _ _ _ _ _ _ _ _

ACT II, SCENE THREE | TRUMP PICKS HIS CABINET

> TRUMP'S OFFICE on another day where CONWAY and TRUMP are mid-conversation.

CONWAY

I agree that celebrating is important, Mister Trump. But you also need to start choosing cabinet positions, sir.

TRUMP

How many do I get to choose, Kellyanne Conway?

CONWAY

You have to choose twenty-two, sir.

TRUMP

I want them all to be made out of solid gold and mounted on the wall of the Oval Office.

CONWAY

Sir?

TRUMP

One of them also needs to be really bigly so that I can fit all of my awards in it. Did you know last year I won the Trump Organization employee of the month thirteen times?

CONWAY

Mister Trump, sir, I'm talking about your government cabinet, not... cabinets.

TRUMP

I do not understand.

CONWAY

Well, the cabinet is made up of the heads of federal executive departments and a few other top advisors.

TRUMP

Like Eric Trump?

CONWAY

No, sir, that's feral.

(CONTINUED)

                         TRUMP
Okay, I want to pick Ivanka Trump, Donald Trump Junior,
Steve Bannon, and Vladimir Putin.

                         CONWAY
I'm not sure that would be appropriate. We don't want to
make it look as though you're only appointing people you
like.

                         TRUMP
What about Jeff Sessions? No one could ever believe that
someone likes Jeff Sessions?

                         CONWAY
Jeff Sessions is good. How about Ben Carlson?

                         TRUMP
It would stop him calling me asking for a job. And we
should try to look diverse.

                         CONWAY
What about Betsy DeVos too? It might be good to get a woman
in there.

                         TRUMP
I like your thinking, Kellyanne Conway.

                    CHRISTIE enters unnoticed.

                         TRUMP
I have to attend an important meeting with Kanye West right
now, can I leave the rest of the decisions to you?

                    TRUMP turns to notice CHRISTIE.

                         CHRISTIE
Hey, Mister Trump.

                         TRUMP
Chris Christie.

                         CHRISTIE
Yes, Mister Trump.

                                             (CONTINUED)

                    TRUMP
I am not choosing you. I know I said we should try to look
diverse, but we do not need to look that diverse.

                    CHRISTIE
Wow, jeez, sir. That really hurts.

ACT II, SCENE FOUR | THE PRESS CONFERENCE

                              A room in TRUMP TOWER where
                              TRUMP is stood behind a podium
                              with CONWAY next to him. In
                              front of them, the ENSEMBLE (as
                              PRESS) sit waiting.

                              At the side of the podium is a
                              table topped with papers and a
                              box.

                    TRUMP
Okay, everyone, I have called this press conference today
to tell you all about the great things I have been doing
since the election and all of the great things that I will
be doing after I am inaugurated next week.
                    (beat)
I will take questions now.

                    PRESS #1
Mister President-Elect, it's been two months since the
election, and this is the first press conference that
you've held. Can you tell us what you've been doing since
November?

                    TRUMP
No, next question.

                    PRESS #5
Mister Trump, could you tell us more about the plans for
your inauguration day? What can we expect to see?

                    TRUMP
Thank you for that question Fox News. I would be happy to
talk about all of the great things that will be happening.
                    (MORE)
                                                  (CONTINUED)

CONTINUED:

                         TRUMP (CONT'D)
You can expect to see so many great things that your mind
will be blown. In the evening more great things will be
happening, and it will be so great and so fantastic. We are
even going to have some fireworks, which will be great, and
do not worry, I have checked the immigration papers of all
of the fire before they started working, okay.

Also, after everyone has left, Paul Ryan, Mitch McConnell,
and Donald J. Trump are going to dismantle all rights for
women using executive orders.

                         PRESS #2
Mister Trump, can I ask you about the pee-pee tape?

                         TRUMP
How do you know about that?

                         PRESS #2
It was mentioned in a leaked dossier that also alleges
Russia helped you to win the election.

                         TRUMP
Neither of those things is true, okay. There is no pee-pee
tape, and Russia did not help me win the election. It is
fake news.

                         PRESS #2
Are you sure, Mister Trump? Because we all got emailed a
link to a password protected movie titled "Trump's Golden
Moments."

                         PRESS #3
It also came with the note, "from Russia with love."

                         PRESS #4
Mister Trump, is this pee-pee tape going to be your
Watergate?

                         PRESS #2
It's going to be his broken-Watergate.

                              The ENSEMBLE laugh as CONWAY
                              whispers to TRUMP.

                                                (CONTINUED)

CONTINUED:

                           TRUMP
Okay, I want all of you to listen because we need to get
some things clear. You are all fake news losers, apart from
you, Breitbart, Fox News and Russia Today, you are all
great and you are doing a fantastic job. But from the rest
of you, I am not going to put up with your fake mainstream
media news. Let me show you something...
                    (choosing someone)
You. Where are you from?

                           PRESS #6
San Fransisco.

                           TRUMP
Then you must be a liberal from M-S-N-B-C?

                           PRESS #6
That's right.

                           TRUMP
Come up here.

                              PRESS #6 stands and moves over
                              to TRUMP.

                           TRUMP
Let us get something clear, okay. You are going to report
as I want you to, and the first thing you are going to
report on is how much work I have been doing. Do you see
all of these papers? You are going to tell everyone that
this is all work and that it is great.

                           PRESS #6
                    (checking the papers)
Mister President-Elect, these are all just blank pieces of
paper. And this box, this is probably empty...
                    (checking inside the box)
There's a horse's head in this box.

                           TRUMP
Casino?... I mean, capiche?

                           PRESS #3
Mister Trump, are you threatening us right now?

                                              (CONTINUED)

PERFORMANCE LICENSE EDITION   LICENSE # _ _ _ _ _ _ _ _

CONTINUED:

> TRUMP

I could kidnap all of your families if that would help?

> PRESS #1

You do know this press conference is being broadcast live, don't you?

> TRUMP

Is it?

> PRESS #1

Yes, Mister Trump, it is.

> TRUMP
> (to CONWAY)

Kellyanne Conway, we are going to need more horse's heads.

> CONWAY

We don't have anymore, Mister Trump, sir. Don't you remember? You used the rest of your horses in Trump Steaks. Does your daughter have any?

> TRUMP

She prefers goats, that is why she married Jared Kushner.

ACT II, SCENE FIVE | AT THE CLINTON'S

> The CLINTON RESIDENCE, where
> CLINTON is mid-conversation on
> the phone.

> NARRATOR
> (entering)

And so it is that on the night before the inauguration, many are feeling sick, scared, and uncomfortable right across the nation. But for some time is scarce to worry, for protests in a flurry are already planned to take place tomorrow right across the land. Meanwhile, in New York's Chappaqua, a small and homely hamlet, Hillary Clinton is wondering why to get out of the inauguration nobody has a plan yet.

> The NARRATOR exits.

(CONTINUED)

                         CLINTON
                       (on phone)
No, I got you, Jimmy. I know it's supposed to be a
tradition for all of us to go, but you know, I've spoken to
W, and he says the seniors are in hospital and being forced
to miss it. Well, we're all old, I'm sure we can catch a
cold or break a leg for the weekend... Oh, you've already
packed the Xanax? I must remember to get some of that.
                       (shouting out)
Hey, Bill, do we have any Xanax?
                       (on phone)
Hey, Jimmy, would it be okay if I was to borrow some of
yours? I'm all out. I'm sure I can bring you something in
return. How about earplugs? Oh, W's sorted those. Alcohol?
No, Barack's on that is he?

                         BILL (OFF)
Hillary.

                         CLINTON
                       (on phone)
I'll work something out. I've got to go now though, Bill's
calling me. We'll catch up properly tomorrow.

                              CLINTON ends her call as BILL
                              enters, looking excited.

                         BILL
Oh, this is going to be the best inauguration day ever.

                         CLINTON
                       (standing)
If you say that again, we're getting a divorce.

                         BILL
But Hillary, it will be. I've found it.

                         CLINTON
Found what? What have you found? Is it a hundred thousand
votes in Michigan?

                              BILL pulls a key from his
                              pocket.

                                              (CONTINUED)

CONTINUED:

                          BILL
This is better. It's my spare key to the White House.

                          Beat.

                          CLINTON
Hey, Bill, do you still have any of those whoopee cushions
left over from the time the D-N-C leadership came over for
dinner?

                                        BILL pulls a whoopee cushion
                                        from his pocket.

                          BILL
That I do, Hillary. That I do. And I've got a whole pile of
photos of us with the Obamas and some strong glue too.

                          CLINTON
I don't say this to you often enough, but William Jefferson
Clinton, I really like you sometimes.

ACT II, SCENE SIX | THE INAUGURATION

                                        THE CAPITOL, Washington, where
                                        the ENSEMBLE (as SPECTATORS) are
                                        gathered for the inauguration of
                                        Donald Trump. Sat among them,
                                        CONWAY, ERIC, IVANKA, JUNIOR,
                                        and SEAN SPICER.

                                        The NARRATOR enters to stand at
                                        the glass podium front center.

                          NARRATOR
The twentieth day of the year's first month, a day which
many in the world hopes will end shortly before lunch. For
today is the day that judgment will fall. Today is the day
that parents will call to tell their children they love
them all.

On Capitol Hill in Washington DC, a breeze blows slowly
over all that's to be.
                          (MORE)

                                                        (CONTINUED)

CONTINUED:

NARRATOR (CONT'D)

And as he prepares to take his spot among those who before him's legacies he'll soon work to rot, friends of his gather among those foes who still matter. While out in the crowds, thousands now stand to shout to him cheers, while walking the streets millions more prepare to scream leers. Three million votes behind, but that's never a fact his supporters will mind, for all they want to see is their new president claiming to be making them free.

Celebration will follow for all those who for Donald they did vote, while a drive to inspire change will fill many more of those who begin to take note.

An inauguration of unity is what many will claim, but days will follow where Barack Obama is still given the blame.

And so as Trump and Pence to this spot they make their way, it's time to begin the ceremony that will keep decency at bay.

MICHELLE (OFF)

Barack, hurry up. You don't want to miss it.

> BILL, CLINTON, and MICHELLE
> enter.

CLINTON

I wouldn't be so sure about that.

MICHELLE

Barack.

> OBAMA enters and joins them.

OBAMA

Oh... my... god...

CLINTON

Hey, where are the Carters?

MICHELLE

They called this morning and said their train has been canceled.

(CONTINUED)

CLINTON
Dang it. Why didn't we think of that?

BILL
What about the Bushes? I was hoping to catch up with W.

MICHELLE
He accidentally booked his flights to the wrong Washington.

OBAMA
Oh... my... god...

                    The four of them take their
                    seats among the crowd.

NARRATOR
And now, please find something to hold on to as we welcome
President-Elect, Donald Trump, and Vice-President-Elect,
Mike Pence.

                    PENCE and TRUMP enter.

TRUMP
Mike Pence, why is your wife not here to watch you today?

PENCE
Oh, Mother said she had an appointment with her doctor
scheduled for today.

TRUMP
What a coincidence. Mary said the same thing to me.

PENCE
Who is Mary, sir?

TRUMP
Number three.

                    Together, they make their way
                    towards the podium and shake
                    hands with the NARRATOR.

                                              (CONTINUED)

CONTINUED:

                              CLINTON hands the NARRATOR a
                              bottle of hand sanitizer.

                         CLINTON
Here, take this.

                              The NARRATOR cleans their hands
                              then hands the bottle back.

                         NARRATOR
Thank you.

                         CLINTON
No problem. Just remember to vote for me in four years. Or
just remember me... please remember me.

                         NARRATOR
                    (to PENCE and TRUMP)
Mister Trump. Mister Pence. If you're both ready, we'll get
started.

                         TRUMP
Before we begin, I do not like the Bible. I prefer people
named Jesus who do not get crucified, and so I have a
different book to swear on.

                              He brings a book from his pocket
                              and shows it to the audience.

                         TRUMP
It is a great book. Such a fantastic read. It is called --

                         NARRATOR
The Art of the Deal by Donald J. Trump.

                         TRUMP
Available now from the failing Amazon dot com, which I hear
is owned by the failing Washington Post loser.

                         PENCE
Such a strong statement, sir.

                         TRUMP
Thank you, Mike Pence.

                                              (CONTINUED)

>   The NARRATOR gestures towards
>   the book.

                         NARRATOR
Mister Pence, would you mind?

>   PENCE takes the book and holds
>   it for TRUMP to place his hand
>   upon.

                         NARRATOR
                      (to audience)
Ladies, gentlemen, and Bill Clinton. We are gathered here
today to mourn the loss of democracy, compassion, decency,
and, most importantly of all, style in the White House.

                         TRUMP
It is going to be so great.

                         NARRATOR
We'll begin with the President-Elect.
                      (to TRUMP)
Donald Jenius Trump, do you solemnly swear that you will
faithlessly embarrass your country on the world stage,
insult and alienate allies, and to the best of your
ability, completely ignore the Constitution of the United
States?

                         TRUMP
So help me, Comrade Vladimir Putin.

                         NARRATOR
Then if nobody has any objections...

>   CLINTON stands, but BILL pulls
>   her down.

                         CLINTON
I've got a few.

                         NARRATOR
Then I do now declare you to be...

                                              (CONTINUED)

CONTINUED:

                              OBAMA
Oh... my... god...

                              NARRATOR
The President of the United States.

                              OBAMA
Wait.

                    Everyone on stage watches as
                    OBAMA stands and makes his way
                    to the podium.

                              OBAMA
If you wouldn't mind, Narrator, I would like to say...
something.

                              NARRATOR
Please go ahead.

                              OBAMA
Thank you.

                    The NARRATOR steps to the side
                    as OBAMA begins to address the
                    audience.

                              OBAMA
Now a lot of people have asked me, ever since the election,
about what I think of the fact that this suntanned turd...
is going to become the President of the United States... I
have not given an answer to that inquiry before, but today,
I am going to give you one... Because the answer is really
quite simple... Let me tell you now that the answer is
yes... yes I do like piña coladas, and I also enjoy...
getting caught in the rain.

                    He rips off his pants to reveal
                    a pair of Hawaiian shorts.

                              OBAMA
                         (to the NARRATOR)
Narrator, my sunglasses if you please.

                                                      (CONTINUED)

                                 The NARRATOR takes a pair of
                                 sunglasses from their pocket and
                                 hands them over.

                          OBAMA
I'm not running things anymore, and that means none of this
crap... is my responsibility.
                    (to MICHELLE)
Michelle.

                                 MICHELLE stands and joins him.

                          OBAMA
We're off to Tahiti to go jet-skiing. Obamas out.

                                 Hand in hand, they both exit. A
                                 beat follows.

                          CLINTON
Well, that was some weird shit.

                                 Beat.

                          TRUMP
Can we move on to Mike Pence now?

                                 PENCE hands TRUMP the book, who
                                 then holds it for him to place
                                 his hand upon.

                          NARRATOR
Of course.
                    (to PENCE)
Michael Richard Pence, do you solemnly swear that you will
accept your fate of being forever remembered by history as
responsible for all of the terrible things that Donald
Trump goes on to do, to not fulfill a single one of your
responsibilities to ensure that the President follows the
law, and to waste thousands of dollars by storming out
sports events that you never wanted to go to in the first
place?

                          PENCE
I do.

                                                    (CONTINUED)
PERFORMANCE LICENSE EDITION   LICENSE # _ _ _ _ _ _ _ _

                          NARRATOR
Then I do declare you to be the Vice-President.

                                        All (except CLINTON and the
                                        NARRATOR) begin to applaud.

                                        Noticing BILL clapping, CLINTON
                                        moves his hands down.

                          BILL
Sorry, Hillary. I just find it emotional.

                          CLINTON
I need to find a bar.

                          NARRATOR
I need to join you.

                                        CLINTON and the NARRATOR exit as
                                        TRUMP takes to the podium.

                          TRUMP
Well, Narrator, thank you very much. President Obama, I do
not know where he has gone. I guess he has to run to the
airport before his visa expires. Also, I would also like to
thank all of those great patriotic Americans who voted for
me.
                    (beat)
Today is a very special day because today we are taking
such great and fantastic power away from Washington, a man
who I hear is overrated, and giving it to Russia.

Throughout this brutal election campaign, ordinary American
voters have told me that they want great things like
schools, they want lots of schools, and also safe
neighborhoods. I have also been told that small business
owners want a strong economy and skilled people to work for
them. But in life, you do not always get what you want. If
they wanted those things, then they should have voted for
Crooked Hillary Clinton.

What I am going to do is make America great again. And to
do this, trust me, such fantastic things will be happening.
                          (MORE)

                                                      (CONTINUED)

CONTINUED:
                          TRUMP (CONT'D)
Everything is going to be so great that you will not even
know that it is great. That is how great it is going to be.

There will be lots of jobs. We are going to create so many
jobs for people like lawyers. So many lawyers, and also
comedians. There is going to be so many lawyers and so many
comedians, that it is going to be like an N-B-C production
office in the year two thousand and ten.
Most importantly of all, I am going to give this country
what it really needs. We are going to have, prepare for
your minds to be blown, a space force. We are going to have
rockets, fast rockets that go whoosh. Also, we will have
some that go wheeee.

For the true patriots of this country, we are also going to
have such a great display of fireworks above our cities on
our Independence Day, June fifth, courtesy of little rocket
man and North Korea.

I know a lot of people are worried right now about the
safety and the security of your family, but to you, I ask a
question, in the event of a nuclear war, would it not be
cool to become a super hero?
                    (beat)
And now, I am going to hand over to Mike Pence.

                              TRUMP stands back as PENCE takes
                              to the podium.

                    PENCE
Well, what are we all standing around for? This is supposed
to be a party. Comrades, let's dance.

ACT II, SCENE SEVEN | THE INAUGURATION PARTY

                              A BALLROOM where in an instant
                              the dress of those on stage has
                              changed to attire of distinctly
                              Russian origin. Equally as
                              Russian is the music now filling
                              the stage.

                                        (CONTINUED)

                              While the ENSEMBLE and others
                              remain on stage, PENCE and TRUMP
                              have disappeared.

                    CONWAY
Comrades, please welcome the President and Vice-President.

                              Synchronized, PENCE and TRUMP
                              return and begin to dance
                              Barynya center stage. Circled
                              around them, their guests clap
                              and cheer as they watch.

                              After a short time, PENCE and
                              TRUMP take a bow together and
                              then move to the side to allow
                              CONWAY and SPICER to take the
                              floor together.

                              Again, those around them clap
                              and cheer for a short while
                              until PENCE and TRUMP join them,
                              and all four dance together.
                              As the music begins to slow, the
                              dancing stops, and all on stage
                              stand arm in arm to sing.

                    ENSEMBLE (EXCEPT TRUMP)
                         (drunkenly)
/DONALD TRUMP IS OUR PRESIDENT, DONALD TRUMP IS OUR MAN. WE
ALL LOVE DONALD TRUMP, HE'S OUR MAN, DONALD TRUMP IS OUR
MAN. HEY!/

                              Silence, and then the music
                              builds once more for ERIC,
                              IVANKA, and JUNIOR to now take
                              center stage.

                              While IVANKA and JUNIOR dance
                              synchronized, however, ERIC
                              stands watching them both
                              confused until eventually he
                              drops the floor and begins to
                              spin himself around.

                                        (CONTINUED)

> As the three of them move to the
> side, next to take the floor is
> a topless PUTIN, who enters by
> cartwheeling from the wings
> before performing a solo.
>
> Finally, as PUTIN finishes, the
> entire stage begins to dance
> together until abruptly, the
> music stops, and the stage
> clears to leave BILL on his own.

                    BILL
I am going to be in so much trouble if Hillary finds out
that I stayed for the party.

ACT II, SCENE EIGHT | THE FIRST PRESS BRIEFING

> The WHITE HOUSE PRESS BRIEFING
> ROOM where the ENSEMBLE (as
> PRESS) sit facing a podium,
> behind which, the NARRATOR
> stands.

                    NARRATOR
With the inauguration over and the party at an end --

> SPICER enters and begins to push
> the NARRATOR away.

                    SPICER
Hey, hey, no. Not your place. Listen here, Narrator person,
I don't know who you are or what you're doing here, but
this is not your show, do you understand? Now get off this
stage before I strangle you with the piece of gum I'm
chewing right now.

> After pushing the NARRATOR
> offstage, he takes his place at
> the podium.

                                          (CONTINUED)

CONTINUED:

SPICER

Okay, now I want all of you son's of bitches to listen up, so I don't have to repeat myself. First up, it's item number one, I have a hangover after the inauguration party last night. It's what big boys and big girls get after they drink alcohol. You'll all learn about that one day.

PRESS #1

Like the morning after impeachment.

SPICER

Right, I heard that. You, what's your name?

PRESS #1

Ayma.

SPICER

That should be Ayma, sir. Do you understand that? Let's try it again, what's your name?

PRESS #1

Ayma, sir.

SPICER

Good, and what's your second name?

PRESS #1

Moron.

SPICER

Ayma Moron.

The ENSEMBLE laugh.

SPICER

Oh, right, I get it. It's a joke. It's joke around with Spicy day, is it? Well, not on my watch. See me in my office at the end of the day. I'm also taking ten points away from C-N-N house for your pathetic attempt to be the joker in the group.

PRESS #2

C-N-N house? Sean, this isn't some sort of school for magic.

(CONTINUED)

CONTINUED:

                              SPICER
Well, you all could have fooled me, that's for sure. I read
all of your reports on the inauguration this morning, and
nearly all of you just conjured up the size of the crowd.
Staying with this, we come to item number two. I'm not
mentioning any names, okay, but I am looking at you when I
say this New York Times. You can't just lie about the
figures to make the President look bad. You were all there,
and you all saw the billions --

                              PRESS #3
Billions, Sean?

                              SPICER
Okay, millions then. Happy now? You all saw the millions of
people who came out to watch the President.

                              PRESS #4
Sean, most of them were protesters.

                              SPICER
Okay, but tell me this, would they have been there if it
wasn't for the President.

                              PRESS #4
They were protesting the President.

                              SPICER
But would they have been protesting the President if it
wasn't his inauguration? Would they have been protesting
Hillary Clinton?

                              PRESS #4
No, they would have been there to celebrate instead.

                              SPICER
Okay, that... that is sort of my point. Here's what's going
to happen, all of you are going to go and write me a new
draft of your inauguration reports using the correct crowd
size figures as homework, even you The Washington Post. I
want all of them on my desk first thing tomorrow, or I will
write home to your parents.

                    PRESS #5 raises their hand.

                                        (CONTINUED)

                          SPICER
Yes, you from Fox News.

                          PRESS #5
Master Hannity sent an apple for me to give you, sir.

                          SPICER
Well, you can tell Sean Hannity that I don't like apples. I
don't go within three feet of any fruit. But it's a nice
gesture, and so I'll tell you what, at recess, you can have
the first choice of toy to play with.

                          PRESS #2
Sean --

                          SPICER
What?

                          PRESS #2
Are you some sort of joke?

                          SPICER
Stop asking questions. The next person who asks me a
question can stand outside until we're done. Okay, we move
on now to item number three. For the stupid among you,
which is all of you, that is one less than four, but one
more than two. It says here that the President will later
today walk from the White House Residence across to the
Oval Office. I don't know what that is so don't ask.
Perhaps it's an office in some sort of Oval shape? I don't
know. Perhaps you can all Google it. To sign some executive
orders with Paul Ryan and Mitch McConnell.

                          PRESS #6
Sean, what will these executive orders be about?

                          SPICER
What did I just tell you all about asking questions? I'm
marking your name down.
                         (beat)
Okay, so it says here that there will be multiple, that
means more than one, executive orders signed that will be
great in nature. So there are some great things going to be
happening, report that, that is your news.
                          (MORE)
                                            (CONTINUED)

CONTINUED:
                          SPICER (CONT'D)
Oh, and it also says that the President will be ordering
people to stop laughing at Mitch McConnell.
                         (beat)
Now during this walk to this circular shaped office, the
President will be joined by his third lady, and I am told
that she will be wearing a long white robe topped with a
wizard-like hat... no, wait, that's going to be the
President. It says Melania will be wearing a bag over her
head because she's embarrassed to be seen with her husband.

                          PRESS #1
Can we report that?

                          SPICER
No. You're all going to report this instead. The First
Lady, Melania Trump, loves... Why aren't you all writing
this down? Get writing before I write it on your faces
using C-N-N's blood for ink.

                    They all begin writing.

                          SPICER
Okay, the First Lady, Melania Trump, loves the President,
that's Donald Trump, very much. The two of them regularly,
and there's a note here that says regularly is at least
three times a week, make love together in the evenings.
Except for the President who makes love five times a week.

                         There's a flash as someone takes
                         a photo.

                          SPICER
Okay, which of you little assholes is taking photos? Was it
you, Washington Post?

                          PRESS #3
My editor asked me to get a photo because you're not
allowing cameras in here.

                          SPICER
Oh, and I suppose that you think you're just going to print
some photo of me in your newspaper with a caption about the
news? Something like this here.
                    (checking his notes)
                          (MORE)
                                                  (CONTINUED)

CONTINUED:

                        SPICER (CONT'D)
Giant Weiner, Sean Spicer, confirms that the President is
not lacking down there.
                        (beat)
I don't want to see another camera. No more photos. Believe
it or not, some of us in this administration don't actually
photograph too well. I'm not mentioning names, but you all
know I'm on about Steve Bannon. And then there's Stephen
Miller, he doesn't photograph at all.

                        PRESS #3
Past administrations have always allowed these briefings to
be broadcast so they can be open to the people.

                        SPICER
This is not a past administration, is it? This is Spicer's
time, and what I say goes. It works like this. The
President decides what the news is, and then he tells me,
Sean Spicer. I then tell all of you what the news is, and
then you go and dumb it down for your readers and your
viewers so that they know what the news is.

                        PRESS #3
What is the news today?

                        SPICER
I haven't had the chance to discuss it with the President
yet.

                        PRESS #1
Sean, did you just call all of our readers and viewers dumb
right now? They are all voters.

                        SPICER
Of course, I'm calling them dumb. Three million more of
them voted illegally for Hillary Clinton rather than our
President, and for some reason, they all decided to vote in
California. I'm not sure what's going on there, but I would
say that's pretty dumb C-N-N.

                        PRESS #4
Can we quote you on that, Sean?

                                                    (CONTINUED)

SPICER
(mocking at first)
"Can we quote you on that, Sean?" How about I quote you on
your dying words as I strangle you with your iPhone
charger? And don't try to pretend you don't all have
iPhones, okay? I know that you liberal fake news people all
use Apple stuff. Siri told me.

PRESS #1
Sean, I really think that the administration has a duty to
show people what they're doing. It's only right that you
allow cameras in here.

SPICER
Well in here it's not what you think that matters. I decide
what happens, the President decides what I decide what
happens, and Comrade Vladimir Putin decides what the
President decides what I decide what happens. It is simple.

PRESS #1
(standing)
I'm sorry, but I think we all have a duty to the people
here. Who's with me?

PRESS #4
(standing)
She's right.

PRESS #3
(standing)
I don't think we should do any more reporting until the
cameras are turned back on.

PRESS #2
(standing)
I think it's time to boycott Sean Spicer.

They all stand, except for PRESS
#5.

SPICER
Oh really? So you're all going to be principled? You're all
going to rally together to stand up to this administration
and make a point?

(CONTINUED)

                         Beat, and they all sit.

                         PRESS #4
Actually, I'm going to leave it to someone else.

                         PRESS #1
I'm sure there are protesters working on this stuff.

                         SPICER
That's what I thought. Okay, we come to item number four
now. The President will, that means he is going to, in a
few days time be hosting a woman from Germany who goes by
the name of... I think it's angled moo-cow.

                         PRESS #2
Sean, do you mean Angela Merkel, the Chancellor of Germany?

                         SPICER
I mean what I said. Don't make me repeat myself.

                         He checks his notes.

                         SPICER
Actually, now that I look at it, it might be Angle --

                         PRESS #2
Angela Merkel?

                         SPICER
Yes, that. Alright, none of you remember that I got that
name wrong, okay. You, C-N-N, are you remembering? I can
see you remembering right now.
                    (beat)
Okay, I think we're done here now. There are some minor
things about banning an entire religion and abolishing all
forms of healthcare, but the details aren't important.

                         He goes to leave as a mumble
                         breaks out.

                         PRESS #3
Banning a religion?

                                             (CONTINUED)

CONTINUED:

                         PRESS #2
Abolishing healthcare? We need more information than that.

                          SPICER
Okay, I want fingers on lips.

                         PRESS #1
What?

                          SPICER
You heard me, fingers on lips.

                              Confused, they do as they're
                              told.

                          SPICER
Are you not all journalists in here?

                              They nod.

                          SPICER
Good, then look up the news and work it out for yourselves.
I'm going for a lie-down.

ACT II, SCENE NINE | MERKEL VISITS THE WHITE HOUSE

                              Remaining in the WHITE HOUSE
                              PRESS BRIEFING ROOM where the
                              ENSEMBLE (as PRESS) remain on
                              stage, now in front of two
                              podiums that stand between a
                              United States flag and a German
                              flag.

                          NARRATOR
                        (entering)
And so as Spicer said in the days ahead, Merkel flew to
meet with the orange guy who when first told he had won
simply said WHO!?. The first world leader to make the trip,
why? Every other had suddenly developed an injury, a four-
year dip. No one wanted to be the first to meet with their
new counterpart who was now the worst.
                         (MORE)

                                             (CONTINUED)

CONTINUED:

                          NARRATOR (CONT'D)
But at the end of the first of her trips, multiple days
filled with multiple blips, a duty she knows she has does
Angela, to straight out the President and to keep her hands
triangular.

                            PRESS #2
Does anyone else feel like we've been here for days?

                            NARRATOR
Ladies, gentlemen, and Fox News of the White House Press
Pool, I present to you the Chancellor of Germany, Angela
Merkel, and President Donald J. Trump.

                              ANGELA MERKEL and TRUMP enter
                              and take their places behind the
                              podiums.

                             TRUMP
Today, I am honored to welcome European President Angel
Murky to the White House.

                              MERKEL begins to drink from a
                              glass of water.

                             TRUMP
I have enjoyed speaking to her today, and I am sure that
she has greatly enjoyed speaking to me too, okay folks.

                              MERKEL spits out her water.

                             MERKEL
I apologize.

                             TRUMP
                        (ignoring MERKEL)
We have a great relationship, and let me tell you, there
has never been a time when our country has had more in
common with Germany.
                          (beat)
I would like now to hand over to Missus Merkel.
                        (to MERKEL)
Chancellor, thank you.

                                            (CONTINUED)

                         MERKEL
Narrator, can you translate?

                              The NARRATOR nods.

                         MERKEL
Thank you.

                              She takes a deep breath.

                         MERKEL
Danke schön, so genannt Herr Präsident.

                         NARRATOR
Thank you very much, so-called Mister President.

                              TRUMP pulls out his phone and
                              begins to play a game on it.

                         MERKEL
Das ist alo der weg, den sie gewählt haben, Amerika?

                         NARRATOR
So this is the path you chose America?

                         MERKEL
Sie haben sich entschieden, den Fanta Fascist zu wählen.

                         NARRATOR
You have decided to elect the Fanta Fascist.

                         MERKEL
Ein wörtlicher großer käse.

                         NARRATOR
A literal big cheese.

                         MERKEL
Ein butterbefeuerter, sonnengebräunter xenophobie mit
händed in der größe von kinderhandschuhen.

                         NARRATOR
A butter-friend, sun-tanned xenophone with hands the size
of children's mittens.

                                          (CONTINUED)

                         MERKEL
Der räuberische rassist des vierten reiches.

                         NARRATOR
The Rapacious Racist of the Fourth Reich.

                         MERKEL
Was zum verdammten wort hast du gedacht, Amerika?

                         NARRATOR
What the naughty word were you thinking, America?

                         MERKEL
Es ist als ob sie zweitausendsechzehn modell brandneue B-M-
W genhandelt haben.

                         NARRATOR
It's as though you traded in brand new two thousand and
sixteen model B-M-W.

                         MERKEL
In glattem schwarz.

                         NARRATOR
In smooth black.

                         MERKEL
Für neunzehnachtunddreißig Volkswagen Käfer in der sonne
orange.

                         NARRATOR
For nineteen thirty-eight Volkswagen Beetle in sunshine
orange.

                         MERKEL
Ernsthaft, der mann ist so dumm, der einzige grund warum er
keinen atomkrieg begonnen hat ist dass er den startcode
nicht buchstabieren kann.

                         NARRATOR
Seriously, the man is so stupid, the only reason he hasn't
started a nuclear war is that he can't spell the launch
codes.

                                              (CONTINUED)

CONTINUED:

                        MERKEL
Sie sind nur eins, zwei, drei, vier, ich erkläre einen
atomkrieg.

                        NARRATOR
They're only one, two, three, four, I declare a nuclear
war.

                        MERKEL
Barack hat es mir gesagt.

                        NARRATOR
Barack told me.

                        MERKEL
                      (with lust)
Oh Barack, vie sehr vermisse ich ihn. Sicher, ich wusste
dass er nicht mehr Präsident sein konnte, aber ich dachte
Hillary würde in der lage sein mit ihm kaffee zu kochen um
über alte zeiten zu reden.

                        NARRATOR
Oh Barack, how I miss him so much. Sure, I knew he couldn't
be president anymore, but I thought that Hillary could set
up coffee with him so we could talk about old times.

                        MERKEL
Obwohl er vielleicht mehr zeit hat, mich zu besuchen. Ich
sagte ihm, Barack, wenn du jemals in Berlin bist, komm und
sag hallo und ich werde dich herumführen. Ich kenne die
besten plätze, wo wir uns hinsetzen und zu mittag essen
können, während die sonne untergeht, während wir uns über
wechselkursmechanismen und außenpolitik im Nahen Osten
unterhalten.

                        NARRATOR
Although he may...
                      (beat, then to MERKEL)
Sorry, could I have that slower?

                        MERKEL
Obwohl er vielleicht mehr zeit hat, mich zu besuchen.

                                          (CONTINUED)

CONTINUED:

                         NARRATOR
Although he may have more time to visit me.

                         MERKEL
Ich sagte ihm, Barack, wenn du jemals in Berlin bist, komm
und sag hallo und ich werde dich herumführen.

                         NARRATOR
I told him, Barack, if you're ever in Berlin, come and say
hello and I'll show you around.

                         MERKEL
Ich kenne die besten plätze, wo wir uns hinsetzen und zu
mittag essen können, während die sonne untergeht, während
wir uns über wechselkursmechanismen und außenpolitik im
Nahen Osten unterhalten.

                         NARRATOR
I know the best places where we can sit down and have lunch
while the sun goes down as we talk about foreign exchange
mechanisms and our policies in the Middle East.

                         MERKEL
Wir hätten so viel Spaß zusammen haben können. Nicht wie
Honky Honky Spaß, nein, ich meine, ha ha, Lachen Sie laut L-
O-L Spaß. ROFL.

                         NARRATOR
We could have had so much fun together. Not like Honky
Honky fun, no, I mean, ha ha, laugh loud L-O-L fun. ROFL.

                         MERKEL
Aber jetzt muss ich mit Trumpelstiltskin über handelsregeln
reden.

                         NARRATOR
But now I've to discuss trade rules with Trumpelstiltskin.

                         MERKEL
Ich habe neulich mit Justin Trudeau telefoniert. Theresa
May denkt nicht viel von ihm, aber ich denke, dass er ein
schöner mann ist. Seine arme sind so stark und er hat ein
gesicht, das mich heiß und verschwitzt macht.

                                              (CONTINUED)

CONTINUED:

                              NARRATOR
I spoke to Justin Trudeau the other day. Theresa May does
not think much of him, bit I think he is a handsome man.
His arms are so strong and he has a face that makes me all
hot and sweaty.

                              MERKEL
Wie auch immer, er sagte, dass er darüber nachdachte,
Donald auf dem G-7—Gipfel im nächsten Jahr den falschen
platz zu nennen, damit wir ihn nicht ertagen mussten.

                              NARRATOR
Anyway, he said that he's considering giving Donald the
wrong location of the G-7 summit next year so we don't have
to endure him.

                              MERKEL
Es wäre immer so ein lustiger witz.

                              NARRATOR
It would be such a fun joke.

                              MERKEL
Ich schätze, ich sollte jetzt der mächtigen mango
zurückgeben, damit er euch alle noch mehr belügen kann.

                              NARRATOR
Well, I guess I should hand back over to the mighty mango
so he can lie to you some more.

                              MERKEL
P-S das pipi ist echt. Ich habe es gesehen.

                              NARRATOR
P-S the pee-pee tape is real. I've seen it.

                              MERKEL
Mister President, over to you.

                                        TRUMP remains focussed on his
                                        phone.

                              NARRATOR
Mister Trump, sir.

                                                      (CONTINUED)

                    TRUMP
                 (looking up)
Oh, is the woman done now? I was playing golf on my phone.
I discovered that if I change the screen settings, I can
make the little man in the game look as orange as me.

                    MERKEL
Er hat auch die gleichen Hände wie du, du komplett
verdammter trottel.

                    NARRATOR
He also has the same size hands as you, you --

                    MERKEL
Actually, don't translate the rest of that. I need a drink
now.

                    She exits.

                    TRUMP
Does that mean I can go too? I want to watch the end of Fox
and Friends while my McMuffin is still warm.

                    The NARRATOR nods and TRUMP and
                    the ENSEMBLE exit.

ACT II, SCENE TEN | COOPER & CONWAY

                    The CNN STUDIO, where COOPER is
                    halfway through interviewing
                    (and arguing with) CONWAY on his
                    show.

                    NARRATOR
It's a fact that in any ordinary circumstances, the meeting
of two world leaders would be the day's news, but it also
remains that Donald J. Trump's opinion of what truly
matters are very different views. And so rather than to
praise the trade the United States from Germany hopes to
graze, he sends on Kellyanne Conway live to defend his
crowd size and popularly dive.

                    The NARRATOR exits.

                                        (CONTINUED)

                              COOPER
I'm just not sure that you actually understand, Kellyanne.
The role of the media and the press is to report the facts,
not to make the President look good.

                              CONWAY
I'm not sure that you're getting it, Anderson. The
President is good, and that's why what he says are the
facts. Why are you seeing to discredit the President?

                              COOPER
I'm not seeking to discredit the President. The President
is discrediting himself, and you're helping him to do that.

                              CONWAY
Well, I don't agree with that. You and the other members of
the liberal mainstream media have been lying about the size
of the inauguration crowd size for days now.

                              COOPER
Why are we back to the crowd size?

                              CONWAY
Do you know how many times Hillary Clinton visited places
like Bowling Green during the election? That small town is
the location of one of this country's worst-ever massacres,
and she didn't go to pay her respects once.

                              COOPER
Kellyanne, what are you on about? There's never been a
massacre in a place called Bowling Green.

                              CONWAY
Okay, it is very disrespectful for you to pretend that
nothing happened, Anderson. But I really don't expect
anything else from C-N-N because none of you care about
lives being lost in Republican states.

                              COOPER
When you're failing to defend yourself, you can't just
change the subject to a made-up massacre and then accuse an
entire network of being disrespectful because no one else
has heard of it.

                                                  (CONTINUED)

                              CONWAY
Actually yes I can do that, Anderson.

                              COOPER
You were on about crowd sizes, I believe?

                              CONWAY
You see, Anderson? It isn't me that's bringing up the
subject of crowd sizes, it's you.

                              COOPER
No, you brought it up and then tried to distract from it by
making something else up.

                              CONWAY
Why do you and C-N-N keep refusing to accept how many
people turned out to celebrate President Trump's
inauguration?

                              COOPER
We prefer to consider the facts, and all of the live
footage from the day shows that turnout was significantly
lower than any previous inauguration.

                              CONWAY
That's not true, and you know it, Anderson. Our Press
Secretary, Sean Spicer, has spent a lot of time trying to
explain the facts to your reporter at the White House, so
how can you still continue to get it wrong?

                              COOPER
Sean Spicer hid in the bushes outside our reporter's house
all night so that he could threaten them with a twig when
they left the next morning.

                              CONWAY
Sure, but after that, he pointed out that millions of
people turned out to see the President.

                              COOPER
Then he was lying.

                              CONWAY
No, he wasn't lying.

                                              (CONTINUED)

                         COOPER
Then what was he doing? Every single factual source proves
that what he was claiming is false.

                         CONWAY
He was giving alternative facts.

                         COOPER
I'm sorry?

                         CONWAY
Sean Spicer was giving alternative facts.

                    COOPER begins to laugh.

                         COOPER
I didn't have any trouble hearing you, Kellyanne.

                         CONWAY
There's no need to laugh, Anderson. You're supposed to be a
professional.

                         COOPER
I don't even know what to say.

                    He laughs harder.

                         CONWAY
That's okay. I know that you understand the truth now.

                         COOPER
It's not that, it's just stupid. It's so stupid.

                         CONWAY
I can wait until you're done. I'm more mature than this,
and I'm going to be the bigger person.

                    COOPER laughs harder still.

                         COOPER
You're on here representing the President of the United
States. What's going on?

                                          (CONTINUED)

>   Laughing even harder, he falls
>   off his chair onto the floor.

                              COOPER
How can any of this be happening?

>   The NARRATOR enters and rushes
>   to COOPER'S side.

                              NARRATOR
Anderson, speak to me, are you okay? Speak to me.

                              COOPER
Everything is just so stupid.

                              NARRATOR
                         (shouting out)
We need help here.

>   The NARRATOR exits before
>   rushing back with a first aid
>   kit, but as they approach COOPER
>   again, they are rugby tackled by
>   PAUL RYAN, who enters at speed.

                              RYAN
                         (to the NARRATOR)
Let me tell you what the problem is here. You want to help
Anderson Cooper, but Anderson Cooper hasn't paid for his
healthcare. Now not only has he collapsed, but he's going
to get worse if you do nothing. We can fix this problem
with a three-pronged approach. Number one, someone is going
to pay for his healthcare. Number two, you are going to
treat him. Number three, I am going to pass a law that bans
all mirrors, so that I never have to look at myself again.

>   RYAN release the NARRATOR as
>   they hand him a bundle of bills
>   from their pocket.

                              RYAN
I don't want to get into the specifics of what just
happened.

                                              (CONTINUED)

                         He exits as the NARRATOR helps
                         COOPER back onto his chair.

                    COOPER
I think that it's time for us to take a commercial break
right now. Thank you, Kellyanne Conway, for joining me.

                         The NARRATOR exits as CONWAY
                         pulls out her phone and begins
                         to dial a number.

                    CONWAY
You know, Anderson, I really think that we're going to have
to rethink our relationship.

                    COOPER
What relationship? I don't want to rethink any relationship
with you. We don't have one, and I want to keep it that
way.

                    CONWAY
I'll talk to you after I've called my husband.

                         She puts the phone to her ear.

                    CONWAY
                     (on phone)
Hey George. Yes, I've just finished my interview with
Anderson Cooper, and I should be home soon. We can have
that special meal we've been planning tonight.
                     (beat)
You know Anderson, he's the one that looks like the love
child of Mike Pence's hair and Andy from Toy Story.

                         A PRODUCTION ASSISTANT enters
                         and hands COOPER a memo before
                         exiting.

                    COOPER
You might want to hold your plans, Kellyanne.

                    CONWAY
What?

                                            (CONTINUED)

CONTINUED:

                         COOPER
And we're live in three, two, one... Hello, and welcome
back to Anderson Cooper three-sixty with me, Anderson
Cooper. Still with me, senior aide to the President,
Kellyanne Conway, who I hope can give us her take on some
breaking news just in. F-B-I director James Comey has, in
the past few minutes, announced that he will be launching a
formal investigation into possible collusion between the
Trump campaign and the Russian Government. Kellyanne...

                         CONWAY
                      (on phone)
George, I'm going to have to call you back.

ACT II, SCENE ELEVEN | THE WHITE HOUSE DAY CARE CENTER

                              A WHITE HOUSE OFFICE where ERIC,
                              KUSHNER, and TRUMP stand holding
                              hands in a circle along with a
                              DAY CARE ASSISTANT.

                         NARRATOR
                      (entering)
With the candlelit dinner at home now to be eaten by George
Conway alone, Kellyanne sets off to the Whitehouse with
haste, the last words from Cooper still leaving a
particularly bad taste. Her boss is now the subject of
multiple questions, and she can't help but worry that to
answer them exactly what will be his suggestions.

But while with ideas of her own in mind she travels, ahead
Donald Trump is ensuring already that any plan just
unravels. For rather than calling his advisors to talk, he
calls in James Comey to tell him to walk. The F-B-I
Director on the spot fired. A move which only by idiots can
ever be admired.

But rather than let just the one man go, where to stop
firing, the President does not know. From an agency head,
and a chief of staff too, each one distracting from the
news that does brew.
                         (MORE)

                                              (CONTINUED)

CONTINUED:

                         NARRATOR (CONT'D)
But how many more departures can he get away with? All why
trying to keep on the truth, his solid gold lid.

                    The NARRATOR exits.

                    DAY CARE ASSISTANT
Okay, so are we all ready to take it from the top again?
One, two, three...

                 TRUMP/ ERIC/ DAY CARE ASSISTANT
/YOU PUT THE RACIST IN, THE RACIST OUT, YOU PUT A RACIST
BACK IN AND DENY WHAT IT'S ABOUT. WHEN THE PRESS ASK
QUESTIONS YOU IGNORE THEM ALL, THAT'S WHAT IT'S ALL ABOUT./

                    DAY CARE ASSISTANT
Very good, Donald. I think you're the best here. Do you
want a verse of your own?

                         TRUMP
/I BROUGHT JAMES COMEY IN, TO MY OFFICE, AND I FIRED HIM, I
FIRED HIM, I TOLD HIM TO GET OUT. I FIRED HIM, AND THEN THE
LOSER RAN, HE SQUEALED LIKE A LITTLE MOUSE./

                    CONWAY enters.

                    DAY CARE ASSISTANT
And who is this joining us? It looks as though we have a
new face. Come in and introduce yourself to the group.

                         CONWAY
Oh, no, I'm not here to join in. I was told the President
was here, and I need to speak to him.

                    DAY CARE ASSISTANT
Well, don't take too long. We're going to start doing some
painting soon.

                 TRUMP approaches CONWAY.

                         TRUMP
What is it you want, Kellyanne Conway?

                                        (CONTINUED)

                              CONWAY
Just some dignity.
                         (beat)
Mister President, what is this place?

                              TRUMP
This is the White House day care center, Kellyanne Conway.

                              CONWAY
How come I've never heard of it before?

                              TRUMP
Why would you have? It is a secret group for top secret
agents. You have to be a big boy to be invited. We even
have codenames. I am Dusty Don, Sean Spicer usually comes,
and his codename is Bushmaster, Jared Kushner is the Silent
Stalker, and Eric Trump is --

                              CONWAY
Is he Eric, sir?

                              TRUMP
Do not be stupid. His codename is Evan.

                              CONWAY
Mister President, I need to speak to you about James Comey.

                              TRUMP
Do not worry about James Comey, Kellyanne Conway. He is
just a pastry chef at the F-B-I.

                              CONWAY
But Mister President, he's just announced that you and your
campaign is now under investigation for working with the
Russian Government.

                              TRUMP
I have already solved it. I fired him.

                              CONWAY lets out an involuntary
                              scream.

                              CONWAY
You fired him, sir?

                                              (CONTINUED)

                        TRUMP
I fired him.

                        CONWAY
Are you not worried that it's going to look like you're
obstructing justice?

                        TRUMP
What is that?

                        CONWAY
Oh, that's where someone's actions actively stop or delay
an investigation or justice being found.

                        TRUMP
I know what obstruction is, Kellyanne Conway. I mean, what
is justice?

                        CONWAY
I may not be the best person to tell you about that.

                        TRUMP
Either way, you are worrying without reason, Kellyanne
Conway.

                        CONWAY
What have you done, Sir?

                        TRUMP
I have fired loads of other people to distract from me
firing James Comey. Someone from the Office of Government
Ethics said it was inappropriate, and so I fired them too.

                        CONWAY
Mister President, this isn't going to look very good.

                        TRUMP
It will be okay. I have you to go and lie out there for me.

                    DAY CARE ASSISTANT
Donald, do you want to come and join us for Twinkle,
Twinkle, Little Star?

                                              (CONTINUED)

CONTINUED:

                        TRUMP
I have to go, Kellyanne Conway.

                                    TRUMP turns away as CONWAY
                                    reaches into her pocket for a
                                    bottle of medication that she
                                    begins to drink from.

                        TRUMP
                     (turning back)
One more thing, Kellyanne Conway. I have also just banned
all Muslims from entering the country.

                        CONWAY
                     (to herself, looking at the
                      bottle)
I'm going to need something stronger.

ACT II, SCENE TWELVE | THE SECOND PRESS BRIEFING

                                    The WHITE HOUSE PRESS BRIEFING
                                    ROOM and the ENSEMBLE (as PRESS,
                                    excluding PRESS #4) sit waiting
                                    in front of a podium.

                        NARRATOR
                     (entering)
Despite the best efforts to distract the President has made
to blur the facts, the press and the public believe still
wary for all of the President's answers feel too airy. For
them, there's something about James Comey's departures that
just doesn't add up, as though there's something being
hidden but ready to come up. And so it is that Sean Spicer
is sent to ensure that the reports of the press are all
equally as bent.

                                    SPICER enters and notices the
                                    NARRATOR.

                        SPICER
Hey, no. I've told you before. Get out!

                                                    (CONTINUED)

CONTINUED:

                              The NARRATOR rushes to exit
                              before SPICER can reach them.

                         SPICER
                    (taking the podium)
Okay. You can shut up. You can shut up. You can shut up.
You can shut up. You especially can shut up, C-N-N, and New
York Times, you can shut up too.

Straight to it, item number one. You all seem to be having
some concerns about the recent staff changes around this
place, but let me tell you, you do not have any concerns,
is that clear? The President can fire who he wants when he
wants, okay.

                         PRESS #1
Sean, he just fired the F-B-I director while he was leading
an investigation into Russia's involvement with the
election and any help that the country offered to the Trump
campaign.

                         SPICER
Maybe you didn't understand it correctly, okay, or maybe
you're just really stupid, I don't know, but the President
did not fire James Comey because he was investigating him.
He fired James Comey because he was very mean to Hillary
Clinton about her emails.

                         PRESS #2
But the President was very mean to Hillary Clinton about
her emails. During the election, he got the crowds at all
of his rallies to shout that she should be locked up.

                         SPICER
Oh, so you finally say that he had crowds at his rallies
now and not a small gathering? Perhaps you can tell your
editor that, New York Times? But no, he didn't do that,
okay. You're making that up or just imagining it or
something.

                         PRESS #2
Sean, it's on tape.

                                              (CONTINUED)

CONTINUED:

                         SPICER
Well, then it's an imaginary tape.

                         PRESS #6
The President also said himself in an interview with Sean
Hannity on Fox News the other day that he fired Comey
specifically because of the investigation and because he
refused to pledge his loyalty to him, something that is now
leading calls for a special prosecutor to be appointed not
only to take over the Russia investigation but also to look
at possible obstruction by the President.

                    They all begin taking notes.

                         PRESS #3
That's a good tip. I didn't have that.

                         SPICER
Seriously, you want to do this, M-S-N-B-C?

                         PRESS #6
I don't understand.

                         SPICER
Okay, you all call yourselves journalists. So how come as
so-called professionals, you're all believing everything
you see on the news?

                         PRESS #6
Sean --

                         SPICER
Just because the President said something on a television
show, it does not make it the truth. Are we clear on that?

                         PRESS #2
But what about the special prosecutor?

                         SPICER
Okay, no more questions. If there are any more questions,
then you'll all be in my office, and last time that
happened to one of you, you didn't leave the same.

                                            (CONTINUED)

CONTINUED:

                         PRESS #1
                         (shaking)
I... I saw things I can't unsee.

                         SPICER
There will be no special pro... damn it.

                         PRESS #6
Prosecutor?

                         SPICER
Yes. There won't be one of those. Period.
                         (beat)
Now, moving on to item number two. The Justice Department
will later today be announcing that they are appointing a
special pro... not again.

                         PRESS #6
Special Prosecutor?

                         SPICER
Yes, that. And I am told to tell you that this will be for
a period, okay.

                         PRESS #2
Sean --

                         SPICER
I said no questions, New York Times. We're going to move on
from item number two to item number three. The President
has appointed a new director of communications who is
starting today. It says here his name is... oh Jesus.

                         PRESS #6
Do you need help?

                         SPICER
No, I do not need help M-S-N-B-C. I can pronounce the name.
It's just, it's --

                    ANTHONY SCARAMUCCI enters.

                                             (CONTINUED)

SCARAMUCCI
Me, Anthony Scaramucci! Hey, thanks for the introduction
there, Spicy, you little son of a bitch. How about we catch
up some time over my favorite dish, amuse-bouche? Or
perhaps we can catch a game, amuse-Mooch! Hey?

SPICER
Okay, that's it. I'm not doing this anymore. I sold the
last remaining bit of my soul and reputation for this job,
and I'm not prepared to now work with the abandoned twin of
some cartoon villain. Spicy is out.

                        SPICER exits as SCARAMUCCI takes
                        the podium.

SCARAMUCCI
Hey, what's that asshole's problem? I'm the Mooch! Everyone
loves the Mooch. Except for my wife, I've just heard she
wants a divorce. Mooch is sad. Poor Mooch.
                (beat)
Hey, okay on to item number four. Steve Bannon sucks his
own cock.

PRESS #2
Can we quote you on that?

SCARAMUCCI
Yeah, why not? I'm the Mooch, and we all want it to be
true, don't we? Okay, item number five. The President has
fired Director of Communications, Anthony Scaramucci.
                (waving)
Well, I'm off to go wrestle Reince Priebus. Hey, Mooch out!

                        SCARAMUCCI exits as SARAH
                        HUCKABEE SANDERS enters and
                        takes the podium.

HUCKABEE SANDERS
Hello there guys. I'm Sarah Huckabee Sanders, and I will be
taking over for Sean Spicer now that he has leaft the
building. Leaft, do you get it? Because he likes bushes.
Okay, item number six. Steve Bannon is also out. Now that's
out of the way, I want to tell you all a story about the
President.
                (MORE)
                                        (CONTINUED)

CONTINUED:
                    HUCKABEE SANDERS (CONT'D)
Once upon a time, there was a little boy called Donald,
that's the President, only guys? Only back then he wasn't
running the country.

                         The ENSEMBLE begins to stand and
                         exit.

                      HUCKABEE SANDERS
Hey, where are you all going? I've not finished my story.
                         (following them)
He was a little boy, of only two hundred and thirty-nine
pounds, and he had a daddy, we all have a daddy, right? We
can relate?...

ACT II, SCENE THIRTEEN | TRUMP FINDS OUT ABOUT MUELLER

                         The OVAL OFFICE, where a large
                         office cupboard now stands next
                         to the desk.

                         The room is empty except for
                         ERIC, who sits alone on the
                         floor, attempting to play a
                         xylophone.

                         NARRATOR
                         (entering)
And so as the news spreads of Mueller's arrival, the
feeling among many is that the ending is final. With a
distinguished career as a veteran and attorney, Robert
Mueller is the man appointed special counsel to end Donald
Trump's journey. But the orange mango who is scared to ever
dance the foreign tango still remains in bliss, for he
watches Fox News' reports on burger emojis that make the
truth easy to miss. But how long can he remain outside the
know? As long as it takes Kellyanne Conway to ruin his
presidential flow.

                         The NARRATOR exits.

                                            (CONTINUED)

CONTINUED:

                         TRUMP
                      (entering)
Okay, Eric Trump, take it from the top. This is going to be
so great.

                    ERIC begins to play.

                         TRUMP
/OH DO NOT GO BREAKING MY NON-DISCLOSURE AGREEMENT./

                         ERIC
/I COULDN'T READ IT IF I TRIED./

                         TRUMP
/OH HONEY DO NOT TELL OUR STORY./

                         ERIC
/I FORGOT MY LINE./

                         TRUMP
/OH DO NOT GO BREAKING MY NON-DISCLOSURE AGREEMENT./

                         ERIC
/ESPECIALLY IF ON DAD YOU PEE./

                         TRUMP
/OH HONEY WHEN YOU KNOCK ON MY DOOR./

                         ERIC
/I FORGOT MY LINE./

            TRUMP   ERIC
/NOBODY KNOWS IT./   /(I DON'T KNOW ANYTHING.)/

                    CONWAY enters as ERIC stops
                    playing.

                         CONWAY
Mister President, sir, and oh, Eric too. I hope that I'm
not interrupting anything important?

                         TRUMP
No, Kellyanne Conway, it is okay. What did you want?

                                              (CONTINUED)

                         CONWAY
It's about the Russia investigation, sir. There's been a
new development.

                         TRUMP
What do you mean, the Russia investigation? There should
not be any Russia investigation. I fried James Comey.

                         CONWAY
Yes, you did, that's the problem. There are quite a few
people, including many in the Justice Department, who think
that you only fired him because he was investigating you.

                         TRUMP
That is fake news. I also fired him because he refused to
pledge loyalty to me, the great Pres...

                         CONWAY
President, sir?

                         TRUMP
Thank you, Kellyanne Conway. Even I find it hard to say
sometimes.

                         CONWAY
You finally have something in common with the world, sir.

                         TRUMP
As I was saying, I also fired him because he refused to
pledge loyalty to me, the great President Donald J. Trump.
Steve Bannon did it.

                         CONWAY
Well yes, but Steve Bannon has also recently left to start
a new job as the interactive trench foot exhibit in a war
museum. Anyway, it sounds crazy, the Justice Department is
using your admission to Sean Hannity that you fired James
Comey over the investigation as evidence that you fired
James Comey over the investigation. They've appointed a
special counsel.

                         TRUMP
Where was Jeff Sessions? Why did he not stop this?

                                              (CONTINUED)

CONTINUED:

> CONWAY
>
> Jeff Sessions couldn't recall why he didn't stop it, but I
> looked into it and found that he was busy selling a new
> range of cookies at the store.

>>> TRUMP moves over to his desk.

> TRUMP
>
> I have a great plan to solve this. I will just fire whoever
> the special counsel is.

>>> He sits, and the sound of a
>>> whoopee cushion deflating fills
>>> the stage before he stands and
>>> holds it up.

> ERIC
>
> Dad made a naughty sound.

> TRUMP
>
> Kellyanne Conway, why is there a whoopee cushion on my
> seat?

> CONWAY
>
> I don't know why, Mister President. Anyway, I'm not sure
> that you can just fire the special counsel. It might not
> look very good, and they've appointed someone who is quite
> influential.

> TRUMP
>
> Who have they appointed, Kellyanne Conway?

> CONWAY
>   (mumbling)
> Robert Mueller.

> TRUMP
>
> Who?

> CONWAY
>
> Robert Mueller, sir.

> TRUMP
>
> Oh no.

                                                    (CONTINUED)

                              Beat, and then TRUMP slowly sits
                              back down on the whoopee
                              cushion.

                    CONWAY
I share your concerns, sir.

                    TRUMP
This is not so great.

                              CONWAY pulls out her phone and
                              begins to look at it.

                    CONWAY
But you might be okay, Mister President. Looking on
Twitter, it doesn't look as though he has any evidence that
you've done anything illegal and **OH GOD!**

                    TRUMP
What is it, Kellyanne Conway?

                    CONWAY
It looks as though he's just found evidence that you've
done things that are illegal.

                    TRUMP
What evidence?

                    CONWAY
Don Junior has just tweeted the messages he received from
Julian Assange last year, and also the guest list for the
meeting with the Russians at Trump Tower.

                    JUNIOR enters.

                    JUNIOR
Hey dad, I was wondering if you could possibly help me out
by signing an executive order to ban some of the hotels
that I don't own.

                    TRUMP
Donald Trump Junior, why did you just tweet about getting
help from Julian Assange and also the Russia meeting?

                                        (CONTINUED)

                        JUNIOR
Oh, well about that... well, I don't know.

                        Beat.

                        ERIC
Hey dad, didn't you tweet about the Russia meeting too?

                              TRUMP pulls out his own phone as
                              ERIC begins to lick his the
                              mallet of his xylophone as
                              though it's a lolly.

                        JUNIOR
                      (to ERIC)
Hey buddy, that thing isn't for eating. It's for playing.
You're supposed to tap it like this.
                      (demonstrating)
Okay, you got it? Now you try.

                        ERIC plays a note.

                        ERIC
It makes a sound.

                        JUNIOR
It does make a sound, yes.

                              As JUNIOR turns away, ERIC
                              begins to tap his own head with
                              the mallet and make a sound each
                              time.

                        JUNIOR
                      (to TRUMP)
Dad, what are you doing?

                              TRUMP looks up from his phone.

                        TRUMP
I am blocking Robert Mueller on Twitter so that he cannot
see what I said about the Russia meeting.

                                             (CONTINUED)

CONTINUED:

                         JUNIOR
Why don't you just delete the tweets?

                         TRUMP
Because blocking people makes me feel excited in a way that
Melania has not made me feel for six years.

                         JUNIOR
You know, I don't think I should have eaten lunch before
coming to see you.

                         TRUMP
It is also fun and just so great to block people, like this
person, because she said that the Pope does not like me,
and this person because they said I upset a cute dog.
Retweeting is also so great, and so I am going to do it now
to this person who says they love what I am doing. Clearly,
they like me so much because they have a cross and a flag
in their bio and have rated me out of ten in their name.
MAGA girl two four nine six eight nine two seven. And now I
also block this person for saying I should delete my
account... oh, I already have Crooked Hillary Clinton
blocked.

                    HUCKABEE SANDERS enters.

                    HUCKABEE SANDERS
Mister President, hello, and hello to everyone else. I've
got a story to tell you all. I was in my office just a few
moments ago when two men arrived with a large package for
you, Mister President, and they wanted to know where to
deliver it.

                         TRUMP
Was it Vladimir Putin. Because I already have enough of
those teddy bears with eyes that move and a microphone for
a nose.

                    HUCKABEE SANDERS
No, sir. Robert Mueller --

                                              (CONTINUED)

CONTINUED:

                           TRUMP
                        (standing)
Quick, Eric Trump, Donald Trump Junior, close the curtains
and barricade all of the doors. Kellyanne Conway, you start
digging us an escape tunnel.

                     HUCKABEE SANDERS
I think you misunderstood me, sir. The package isn't Robert
Mueller, it's just from Robert Mueller. He sent it.

                           CONWAY
Mueller sent it? But what is it?

                     HUCKABEE SANDERS
I don't know, Kellyanne.

                           TRUMP
Have it brought in here.

                                 HUCKABEE SANDERS exits and then
                                 returns a moment later with two
                                 DELIVERY MEN carrying a large
                                 and flat wrapped package.

                           TRUMP
                    (pointing at his desk)
Place it on here.

                                 After doing as instructed, the
                                 DELIVERY MEN exit as TRUMP
                                 unwraps the package, and all
                                 (except ERIC) gather around.

                           JUNIOR
So you know, that looks like a portrait.

                                 TRUMP holds it up to show a
                                 portrait of Robert Mueller.

                           CONWAY
Okay, so does anyone think that it's suspicious that Robert
Mueller is sending a portrait of himself?

                                                  (CONTINUED)

CONTINUED:

                         TRUMP
Clearly, he is just sending it to show that there are no
hard feelings between us. He is a smart man, Kellyanne
Conway, and smart men often sent portraits of themselves to
show that they are smart.

                         CONWAY
I'm still suspicious of it, sir.

                         TRUMP
                    (ignoring CONWAY)
I think that it would look so great on this wall here.

                              He takes the portrait and puts
                              it up on the wall behind his
                              desk.

                         TRUMP
And now he can sit over me as my guardian angel of not
being under investigation.

                              As they all turn away from the
                              portrait, it 'opens' as if a
                              door and the real ROBERT MUELLER
                              appears and begins to listen to
                              the conversation.

                         CONWAY
But, Mister President, you are under investigation.

                         MUELLER nods.

                         TRUMP
Wrong. Robert Mueller would not have sent me a present if I
was under investigation.
                    (to JUNIOR)
Donald Trump Junior, can you go and get Mike Pence?

                         JUNIOR
Sure. I'll go get him for you right now.

                         JUNIOR exits.

                                             (CONTINUED)

CONTINUED:

                          CONWAY
Mister Trump, I really think you should be talking to a
lawyer.

                          TRUMP
Okay, if you insist, Kellyanne Conway --

                              TRUMP turns to the cupboard next
                              to his desk as PENCE enters
                              wearing ear muffs.

                          PENCE
Mister President, sir. You asked to see me.

                          TRUMP
Mike Pence, why are you wearing ear muffs?

                              PENCE remains silent, and so
                              TRUMP walks over and lifts off
                              his ear muffs.

                          TRUMP
Mike Pence, I said, why are you wearing ear muffs?

                          PENCE
Because my lawyer advised me to wear them whenever I am
around you. He said that if I can't hear what you're
saying, then it's much easier to plead innocent.

                              PENCE puts the ear muffs back
                              on.

                          TRUMP
Mike Pence, we need your help.

                          Beat.

                          PENCE
I would love to stay and catch up with all of you, but if
none of you mind, I have my inauguration to start planning.

                          PENCE exits.

                                              (CONTINUED)

CONTINUED:

                         TRUMP
Do you think he will invite all of us?

                         CONWAY
Mister Trump, you've got more important things to worry
about.

                         TRUMP
Quite right, Kellyanne Conway.

                              TRUMP turns back to the
                              cupboard.

                         CONWAY
What are you doing, sir?

                         TRUMP
I am calling Michael Cohen. Michael Cohen.

                              The cupboard shakes for a moment
                              then goes still before COHEN
                              walks out of it.

                         COHEN
You called, boss?

                              CONWAY and HUCKABEE SANDERS
                              watch in shock while ERIC points
                              with wonder.

                         ERIC
Magic trick.

                         CONWAY
What were you doing in a cupboard?

                         COHEN
Oh, it's where I live now, Kellyanne. I had to sell my
house to help get the boss out of some trouble.
                    (to TRUMP)
Nasty business with Robert Mueller. I've just heard more
news too, he's got Paul Manafort, the guy's in jail right
now.

                                        (CONTINUED)

CONTINUED:

                         TRUMP
Who is Paul Manafort?

                         CONWAY
He used to get the coffee around here before I started.

                         TRUMP
Kellyanne Conway, go and send his family some flowers for
their loss, and also work on convincing one of his children
to start a fire in his filing cabinet.

                         CONWAY
I'll get straight to it, Mister President.

                    CONWAY exits.

                         TRUMP
So, Michael Cohen, what is your plan to get me out of this
investigation?

                         COHEN
I'm still working on coming up with something. Perhaps you
should consider hiring another lawyer to help?

                         TRUMP
I am already ahead of you, Michael Cohen.
                    (to HUCKABEE SANDERS)
Sarah Huckabee Sanders, can you go and find me Rudy
Giuliani?

                    HUCKABEE SANDERS
I can certainly do that for you, Mister President. It
sounds like it could be the start of a great adventure.

                 HUCKABEE SANDERS exits.

                         COHEN
About another matter, though, boss. I got a call earlier
from a guy. He claims to be a lawyer representing a Stormy
Daniels. You know, that porn star that you fu --

                         TRUMP
Michael Cohen, I am going to have to stop you there. There
is a child in the room.

                                        (CONTINUED)

                         COHEN
That porn start whose... missus Eric you stuck your mister
Eric in.

                         ERIC
Hey, that's an Eric kiss.

                         MUELLER coughs, and they look at
                         him.

                         MUELLER
Excuse me.

                         TRUMP
You are excused, Mister Robert Mueller.

                         They look away from Mueller.

                         COHEN
Anyway, boss, this guy said they're getting ready to sue
you because you never signed a non-disclosure agreement
with her.

                         TRUMP
That is fake news. I always sign non-disclosure agreements.
The only one that I have not signed is the one you gave me
before my speech last year, which I have right here...

                         He pulls the agreement from one
                         of the desk draws and begins to
                         look through it.

                         TRUMP
And this one is between Donald J. Trump and... what does
this say here, Michael Cohen?

                         COHEN moves closer.

                         COHEN
Stormy Daniels. It says Stormy Daniels and you forgot to
sign it. You told me that you never forgot to sign
anything.

                                              (CONTINUED)

                        TRUMP
I do not remember saying that.

                        COHEN
Well, this could be a big problem, boss. This guy is a bald
guy, and no Breitbart reading kind neither. He may turn out
to be nearly as crooked as you some day, but he's got real
certificates. Not just those you get printed from some word
processor when you graduate Trump U.

                        TRUMP
Okay, we need a plan.

                    RUDY GIULIANI enters.

                        GIULIANI
Well, if you need a plan, then I am your man.

                        TRUMP
Rudy Giuliani.

                        GIULIANI
That's my name, and let me tell you... /YOU'VE GOT TROUBLE,
RIGHT HERE IN THIS OFFICE, I'M TALKING TROUBLE WITH A
CAPITAL T WHICH ALSO STANDS FOR TREASON./
                        (beat)
/BUT DON'T YOU WORRY, FOR SIR I HAVE A PLAN, WE'RE GOING TO
SAY TO EVERYONE ASKING THAT YOU'RE GUILTY./

                        TRUMP
I do not understand.

                        GIULIANI
/WE'RE GOING TO SAY THAT YOU'RE GUILTY./

                        COHEN
That he's guilty?

                        GIULIANI
/THAT HE'S GUILTY. WE SAY IT SO MUCH WE CONFUSE THEM ALL
INTO THINKING YOU'RE NOT./

                        COHEN
Into thinking that he's not guilty?

                                        (CONTINUED)

PERFORMANCE LICENSE EDITION   LICENSE # _ _ _ _ _ _ _ _

                         GIULIANI
/THAT'S RIGHT./

                          TRUMP
Why are you singing

                         GIULIANI
It's supposed to be a musical.

                          COHEN
No. It's supposed to be an alternative musical.

                          Beat.

                          COHEN
Boss, we still need to come up with a plan that might
actually work.

                         GIULIANI
I've just said, we're going to say he's guilty.

                          COHEN
But will it work, though?

                          TRUMP
Rudy Giuliani, will it work?

                         GIULIANI
Well, we've been saying it about Hillary Clinton for years,
and she's still not in jail.

                          TRUMP
Okay, Rudy Giuliani, I want you to go on all of the fake
news tonight and tell them that I am guilty. Michael Cohen,
I want you to take a shower because you smell like a not so
great bag of fried chicken, and then I want you to sort out
this Stormy Daniels problem.

                         GIULIANI
That's it, Donald, you've got it.

                          COHEN
Sure thing, boss.

                                              (CONTINUED)

CONTINUED:

                              As COHEN and GIULIANI exit,
                              TRUMP turns back to ERIC.

                         TRUMP
Okay, Eric Trump, whenever you are ready.

                              ERIC begins to play.

                         TRUMP
/AND I THINK IT IS GOING TO BE A SHORT, SHORT TIME,
'TILL MUELLER INVESTIGATES ME AND FINDS,
I AM NOT THE MAN MY VOTERS THINK IS INNOCENT,
OH, NO, NO, NO. KIM JONG UN IS A ROCKET MAN.
SHORT, AND FAT, BURNING UP HIS COUNTRY ALL ALONE.../

                              TRUMP exits as MUELLER looks
                              down at ERIC and begins to
                              smile.

ACT II, SCENE FOURTEEN | MUELLER INTERROGATES ERIC

                              OUTSIDE THE WHITE HOUSE where a
                              toy car is parked.

                         NARRATOR
                        (entering)
It would be true to say that across the administration, the
level of intelligence is not so high, but for one member,
it's lower and all who see him only sigh. But maybe his
family believe his heart is in the right place, even if he
struggles daily to tie up his own shoelace. Or perhaps it
is that he has to stay for he knows too much, a possibility
that some want to know if the case truly is as such. Eric
Trump has been the kid who has sat through every meeting
and seen exactly who his father has been greeting. But is
he loyal to his family name? Or can Robert Mueller use him
to his investigation's gain?

                              ERIC enters and climbs into the
                              car before he begins pushing
                              himself around the stage, making
                              engine noises.

                                             (CONTINUED)

CONTINUED:

                              After a moment, the NARRATOR is
                              joined by two FBI AGENTS, and
                              together, they sneak up behind
                              ERIC and push the car offstage.

                    ERIC (OFF)
Hey, where are you taking me? I'm the dumb one.

                              Lights out, and for a moment,
                              nothing, until a single
                              spotlight goes up on ERIC on sat
                              sitting opposite a desk.

                    ERIC
What's going on? I can see the light. Am I dead? I feel
like this looks like how dad describes a date.

                    FBI AGENT #1 (OFF)
Are you Eric Frederick Trump?

                    ERIC
No. I'm just Eric.

                    FBI AGENT #2 (OFF)
Are you the son of President Donald J. Trump?

                    ERIC
He prefers if we call him Lord Führer at home.

                              The stage lights up to reveal an
                              interrogation room.

                              ERIC looks around as footsteps
                              grow in volume until the two FBI
                              AGENTS enter along with ROBERT
                              MUELLER.

                    MUELLER
Mister Trump...

                              He goes to shake ERIC'S hand,
                              but rather than reciprocate,
                              ERIC grabs and licks his.

                                        (CONTINUED)

                         MUELLER
Mister Trump, I am Robert Mueller.

                    He sits opposite ERIC.

                          ERIC
Son of a bitch.

                         MUELLER
I'm sorry?

                          ERIC
That's what dad calls you.

                         MUELLER
Well, that's who I wish to speak to you about today, Mister
Trump.

                          ERIC
I'm not allowed to talk to strangers.

                         MUELLER
Don't think of me as a stranger. Think of me as a distant
but kind uncle of yours.

                          ERIC
Can I have some candy?

                         MUELLER
I'm not sure I understand you, Mister Trump.

                          ERIC
I want candy. Uncles give candy.

                         MUELLER
Okay, I'm not that sort of uncle. I just want to ask you a
few questions and get a few answers.

                          ERIC
Can I have candy after?

                         MUELLER
                     (to FBI AGENTS)
Does either of you have some sweets we can give this kid?

                                        (CONTINUED)

                              One of them reaches into their
                              pocket and pulls out a bag of
                              M&Ms to hand to ERIC.

                    FBI AGENT #1
I've only got these, sir.

                    ERIC
Uncle Mueller, I'm not allowed candy.

                    MUELLER
Well, I'm letting you have them as a special treat. Think
of me as a naughty uncle that lets you do things you
normally wouldn't be allowed to do.

                    ERIC
Like when dad asks Ivanka to call him an uncle, so it
sounds less creepy?

                    MUELLER
Mister Trump, I'm going to need you to swear an oath right
now that you're going to tell us the truth.

                    ERIC
I can't do that, Uncle Mueller. Junior says it's bad to
swear.

                    MUELLER
Look, Mister Trump, I just want to ask you about your
father and what he did during the election last year, and I
need you to promise that you'll tell the truth.

                    ERIC
Can we go eat pizza and watch a movie after?

                    MUELLER
Mister Trump, if you help us out here, then I promise that
I will personally arrange for you to meet the star of your
favorite movie.

                    ERIC
Cool. I've always wanted to meet a talking snowman.

                                             (CONTINUED)

CONTINUED:

                         MUELLER
So do we have an arrangement?

                         ERIC
Okay, but I can't tell you about any of the stuff that dad
said I'm not allowed to talk about.

                         MUELLER
What did he say that you're not allowed to talk about?

                         ERIC
The help he got from the Russia meeting, Vladimir Putin
voting multiple times in Wisconsin, fake news online
attacking Hillary Clinton, and WikiLeaks hacking the D-N-C
for him.

                         MUELLER
Is there anything else he said you can't talk about?

                         ERIC
Future mom.

                         MUELLER
Who is future mom?

                         ERIC
She's the porn star that dad has Eric kisses with. But he
doesn't want anyone to know about her because his Uncle
Cohen paid her one hundred and thirty thousand dollars to
stay quiet.

                         MUELLER
One hundred and thirty thousand dollars? Why doesn't he
just use the internet like everyone else?

                         ERIC
Sometimes they only get paid one hundred and twenty
thousand.

                         Beat.

                                              (CONTINUED)

CONTINUED:

                         MUELLER
                     (to FBI AGENTS)
This kid is so stupid, I don't know whether to punch him or
kiss him for making our job easier.

                          ERIC
Don't kiss me. The doctor said it might be contagious.

                         MUELLER
Now, Mister Trump, you love your father, right?

                          ERIC
What is love?

                         MUELLER
Oh, love... well, love is what the majority of Americans
will be feeling towards me when I wrap up this
investigation.

                          ERIC
Will anyone ever feel love towards me?

                         MUELLER
I'm sure we can get you a pet if you want to try to
experience it yourself.

                          ERIC
No. I don't want a Reince Priebus.

                         MUELLER
I don't follow you, Mister Trump.

                          ERIC
That's what Uncle Scaramucci always called him. I miss
Uncle Scaramucci, but dad said he had to go away to a
better place.

                         MUELLER
I don't want to interrupt your story, Mister Trump, but I'd
quite like to wrap up this interview soon. So, I'm going to
ask you again, do you love your father?

                          ERIC
I think so.

                                          (CONTINUED)

                          MUELLER
Very good, that makes this easier. Now, there's a very good
chance that he's soon going to be locked up for a very long
time, do you understand me?

                          ERIC
Is that like when he asks Ivanka to bring the chains?

                          MUELLER
Back to your father being in jail, Mister Trump. I'm sure
that if you loved him, you wouldn't want him to be alone
for the rest of his life, would you?

                          ERIC
No, but he could just get a mirror. That's what I do when I
want a friend to play with. I'm not talking to that friend
anymore, though. He said I look funny.

                          MUELLER
Well, what we want to arrange for your father is something
similar to that, only with real people. His friends and his
family, for example. So can you help us out with that, so
he isn't alone?

                          ERIC
Sure.

                          MUELLER
So who do you think we should lock up with him for the
company? Anyone who has similar interests to him like
treason and sexual assault?

                          ERIC
Well, there's Jared Kushner and Donald Trump Junior.

                              MUELLER begins to note the names
                              down.

                          ERIC
Michael Cohen, Kellyanne Conway, Sean Spicer, Vladimir
Putin, Ivanka Trump, Eric Trump, Michael Flynn, Stephen
Miller, Steve Bannon, Rudy Giuliani, Jeff Sessions,
European mom, and a some guy named George.

                                              (CONTINUED)

CONTINUED:

                         Beat.

                         MUELLER
                    (to FBI AGENTS)
Look at this kid.
                    (to ERIC)
Well, Mister Trump, that's all that I need to ask you.
You've been a big help to me and your country.

                         ERIC
Do I get to meet a talking snowman now?

                         MUELLER
Meet a talking snowman?... Well, I'll tell you what, if you
come back here next week, you can meet one, okay? But just
remember to bring your father and your brother too, you
wouldn't want them to miss out now, would you?

                         ERIC
What about Jared Kushner?

                         MUELLER
Now you're getting it. Well, run along then and tell them
all the exciting news.

                         ERIC
Thank you, Uncle Mueller. I love you.

                         MUELLER
And right now, I love you too, kid.

                         ERIC begins walking offstage.

                         MUELLER
The exit is the other way, Mister Trump.

                         ERIC
I knew that.

                         He changes direction and exits.

                         MUELLER stands and puts his arms
                         around the FBI AGENTS.

                                        (CONTINUED)

                         MUELLER
You know, I think we can go out and celebrate tonight. I
think we've got those treasonous assholes.

ACT II, SCENE FIFTEEN | MICHAEL COHEN FLIPS

                              The OVAL OFFICE, where JUNIOR
                              sits tied to a chair while TRUMP
                              is taunting him by holding
                              hairspray just out of reach.

                         NARRATOR
                        (entering)
With now in hand the knowledge that from Eric Trump he did
demand, Robert Mueller sets forth to have his team raid
offices from the south, east, west, and to the north.
Lawyers, secretaries, and a tea boy too, Flynn, Manafort,
and Michael Cohen, to name just a few. The net is now
closing fast around the President, and many around him know
exactly by this what is meant. Every other day a new name
jumps ship, and with a lifeboat ready sits Mueller if they
promise to talk from their lip. But with a team of lawyers
working to work the lies which they mill, Donald Trump sits
confident of being found innocent somehow even still. Sure
his son Junior shared on Twitter evidence and more, but
that is why now he sits tied to a chair on the Oval Office
floor. For his father to solve it is still sure of his
plan, but then still little does he know he's about to lose
his favorite lawyer man.

                         The NARRATOR exits.

                         TRUMP
You are not getting your hairspray back until you have sent
that tweet, Donald Trump Junior.

                         JUNIOR
But dad, if I don't spray my hair at least once an hour,
then I end up looking like you.

                                            (CONTINUED)

CONTINUED:

                         TRUMP
Then pull out your phone and get tweeting, otherwise I will
leave you tied up and make you babysit your brother
tonight, and just a little F-Y-I, we have not changed his
diaper.

                         JUNIOR
Okay, fine.

                    He pulls out his phone.

                         JUNIOR
                    (to himself, reading)
"I welcome this opportunity to share this statement to set
out the circumstances around the reported Russia meeting at
Trump Tower last year."
                    (to TRUMP)
What do you want me to say?

                         TRUMP
It has been reported by the lying fake news media that I
met with Russia. I did meet with Russia, but nothing
happened, and I did not do anything illegal. If I did do
anything illegal, then it was the fault of Crooked Hillary
Clinton. P-S, my father was not at the meeting.

                    COHEN enters.

                         COHEN
You know, boss, you're wasting your time. There's no point
in trying to fight it.

                         TRUMP
What are you talking about, Michael Cohen?

                         COHEN
I'm talking about how it's not going to make a difference.
Everyone already knows about that Russia meeting and
everything that happened at it. You tweeted about it, Don
Junior tweeted about it, and Comrade Putin even set a photo
from it as the header of the Kremlin's profile.

                                           (CONTINUED)

                              TRUMP
I am not worried, Michael Cohen. We are just going to deny
the Russia meeting, and then they have no more evidence.

                              COHEN
I wouldn't be sure of that, boss. Last I heard, Robert
Mueller sat down with one of your children the other day
and asked some questions.

                              TRUMP
None of them would be stupid enough to have told the truth.

                              COHEN
It was Eric Trump.

                         Beat.

                              TRUMP
We are so screwed.

                              COHEN
Exactly, boss. Robert Mueller now has all the evidence he
needs.

                              TRUMP
I still do not need to worry. I still have you as my
lawyer, and as long as you are here, there will always be
someone to pay the bribes to get me out of any situation.

                              COHEN
Well actually, about that, boss. I've come to hand in my
resignation to you. I've been speaking to the Mueller team,
and they've offered me an out. I want to flip.

                              TRUMP
You do not get an out, Michael Cohen. No one in this
administration gets a way out. There are no redemptions
from this.

                         GIULIANI enters.

                              TRUMP
Rudy Giuliani, have you heard this? Michael Cohen says he
is going to flip.

                                        (CONTINUED)

CONTINUED:

                         GIULIANI grabs COHEN by the
                         head.

                         GIULIANI
I'm sure he's just having a joke with us.

                         COHEN
Hey, get off me. I'm not joking around here.

                         COHEN breaks free.

                         COHEN
They came and raided my office this morning and found
evidence of everything. There's nothing more I can do for
you now, and I don't think there's anything you can do
either, boss.

                         TRUMP
What are you saying, Michael Cohen?

                         COHEN
I'm saying that right now, I'm pretty sure there's a Stormy
coming right for you.

                         Beat.

                         TRUMP
Please, Michael Cohen. There must still be something that
you can do for me?

                         COHEN
Mister Trump, I'm not even a real lawyer. I couldn't even
get a place at Trump U. I had to get my degree from Trump U
Junior.

                         TRUMP
I can offer you money. I can offer you lots of great green
American dirty bribe money.

                         COHEN
Boss, you still haven't paid me back for paying off all
those lawsuits for you. Besides, Robert Mueller has offered
me something you never could.
                         (MORE)

                                              (CONTINUED)

CONTINUED:

                          COHEN (CONT'D)
A nice comfortable cell where I get three meals a day, new
clothes, and never have to speak to another member of the
public ever again.

                            TRUMP
Please, Michael Cohen. Stay and help me.

                            COHEN
No, Mister Trump. This is the end. It's over. You've never
respected me, and the other lawyers bully me --

                           GIULIANI
That's not true.

                            COHEN
Yes, it is. You always steal my lunch money, and you even
wrote to the President of the Bar Association to tell her I
have posters of her on my bedroom walls.

                           GIULIANI
It was a good joke.

                            COHEN
I don't even have a bedroom. I have to live in a bush now
because the boss evicted me from my cupboard.

                            TRUMP
It was prime real estate, Michael Cohen. You know that.

                            COHEN
Have you got any idea what it's like to have Sean Spicer as
a roommate?

                            TRUMP
What about if I give you your cupboard back?

                            COHEN
It's too late. Robert Mueller is going to bring you and
everyone around you down. And you know what, I'm going to
help them as much as I can. You're a bad man, Mister Trump,
and everyone is going to find out what you've done to their
country. You're not the boss of me anymore... boss.

                                             (CONTINUED)

CONTINUED:

>   Beat, and then COHEN exits as
>   CONWAY and ERIC enter.

                    CONWAY
Mister President, do you need a moment? That looked as
though it was emotional.

                    TRUMP
Kellyanne Conway, we just lost a very fine, and a very
great, member of our catering team.

                    CONWAY
Well anyway, sir, I think that we're going to need to come
up with a new idea.

                    GIULIANI
What's wrong with my idea? It's working. We've told
everyone that the President is guilty and he's not been
arrested yet.

                    CONWAY
Yet.

                    GIULIANI
They can't arrest a sitting president. They wouldn't try.

                    CONWAY
No, but they can wait until he's not a sitting president.
And they can also arrest all of us now.

                    GIULIANI
Then we will them that we're all guilty. That everyone is
guilty. What are they going to do about it? Arrest all of
us?

                    CONWAY
They are trying to. Just last week, they indicted twelve
household cleaners, eleven gardeners gardening, ten lawyers
lying, nine drivers driving, eight butlers buttling, seven
librarians reading, six stewards seating, five-clothes-
valets, four table waiters, three bell boys, two tea
blenders and the former campaign barista.

>   ERIC begins to clap.

>   (CONTINUED)

CONWAY
(to ERIC)
Thank you.
(to TRUMP)
So you see, sir, I really think we need to try doing
something different.

TRUMP
Have we tried calling it all a witch hunt in the hope that
it makes it just go away? Or we use thoughts and prayers?

CONWAY
We only use thoughts and prayers for problems we could
actually fix if we wanted to, sir.

TRUMP
What about paper towels? Have we tried paper towels?

CONWAY
Paper towels don't really do anything, sir... ever.

TRUMP
What about Jeff Sessions? Why can't he just close down the
investigation?

CONWAY
Oh, about Jeff Sessions. I saw him earlier, and he said he
was planning on coming to see you, but he's going to have
to reschedule because he's got to spend the day trying to
recall which rainbow he left his pot of gold at the end of.

Also, Mister President, if you don't mind me asking, why is
Donald Trump Junior tied to a chair?

JUNIOR
Can someone untie me now?

TRUMP
I cannot let you out, Donald Trump Junior. I used a lock
and gave the key to Eric Trump to keep it safe.

They all look to ERIC.

(CONTINUED)

CONTINUED:

                              ERIC
That was a key? I thought it was candy.

                     KUSHNER enters.

                             CONWAY
So what are we going to do about Robert Mueller, sir?

                              TRUMP
Jared Kushner, do you have any ideas?

                     KUSHNER holds up a cue card.

                             CONWAY
                          (reading)
"No. I have no idea about anything and don't know why I'm
still here."
                          (beat)
Jared Kushner has no idea about anything and doesn't know
why he's still here, sir.

                              ERIC
Why don't we just run away?

                            GIULIANI
The kid has a point. Running away could work.

                              TRUMP
Kellyanne Conway, what language do they speak in South
America?

                             CONWAY
They speak Spanish in many places, sir. Why do you ask?

                              TRUMP
Puedo hablar Español.

                             CONWAY
Mister President?

                              TRUMP
I said I can speak Spanish. My father taught it to me when
I was a little boy and told me that if I ever get into
trouble, then I should run away to South America.

                                        (CONTINUED)

                    CONWAY
But what about your children, sir?

                    JUNIOR
Yo tambien puedo hablar Español.

                    TRUMP
Donald Trump Junior and Ivanka Trump are both fluent. Even
Eric Trump knows some words.

                    ERIC
Guten tag.

                    CONWAY
Mister President, are you suggesting that we just leave all
of this behind? That we just run away from the mess we've
created so that someone else has to clean it up?

                    TRUMP
Yes, I am.

                    CONWAY
I'm in. What do we do?

                    TRUMP
Rudy Giuliani, I need you to stay behind and make sure that
no one knows we have gone anywhere.

                    GIULIANI
I can do that, and when they come after me, I'll just tell
them that I'm guilty. What's the worst they can do?

                    CONWAY
Prosecute you for treason.

                    GIULIANI
They only prosecute you if they like you, Kellyanne.

                    TRUMP
Donald Trump Junior, you are going to stay tied to that
chair until we can get the key back.

                                              (CONTINUED)

                         JUNIOR
Why can't we just tell Eric where babies come from so he
brings it back up straight away?

                         ERIC
I already know where babies come from. The baby fairy puts
them under your pillow at night.

                         TRUMP
                    (to JUNIOR)
Because no one wants to clean up that mess.
                    (to CONWAY)
Kellyanne Conway, I need you to go and get Ivanka Trump,
and also some glasses and some fake mustaches, and then
meet us at the airport in one hour.

                         CONWAY
Mister President, just one thing, sir. I really like this
plan, okay, but don't we need to leave someone behind to
take the blame for us.

                         TRUMP
Kellyanne Conway, I have already thought about this, and I
know of such a great goat.

                              Slowly, they all turn to stare
                              at KUSHNER, who, after staring
                              back for a moment, turns around
                              his cue card to reveal, "Why are
                              you all looking at me?"

ACT II, SCENE SIXTEEN | THE ESCAPE TO SOUTH AMERICA

                              An AIRPORT TERMINAL where
                              CONWAY, ERIC, IVANKA, and TRUMP,
                              along with JUNIOR (still tied to
                              a chair), all of them are
                              wearing glasses and a fake
                              mustache, are talking to a CHECK-
                              IN agent.

                                             (CONTINUED)

NARRATOR
(entering)
And so with Cohen having flipped, next comes the inevitable sinking of the ship. The days of freedom are now limited for those at the top, and they know they have no choice but to flee from the chop. Donald J. Trump with two of his sons and Ivanka too, along with Kellyanne Conway, who completes their few. Mike Pence has already fled the nest, and not one of them cares who is arrested from the rest.

The NARRATOR exits as HANNITY enters but stands to watch from the side.

TRUMP
Hello check-in person, we are here for the flight to South America even though I hear it is overrated. There is five of us.
(looking around)
Make that four of us, we should probably check Donald Trump Junior in as baggage because we still cannot untie him.

ERIC
I haven't been for poo-poo yet.

CHECK-IN AGENT
And do any of you have a preference of where you'd like to sit on the plane?

TRUMP
As far along the right-wing as possible.

CHECK-IN AGENT
And other than this chair, do you have any baggage to check?

CONWAY
I might need to pay some excess charges here. I've picked up a lot since I started working for Mister Trump.

The CHECK-IN AGENT hands over their boarding passes.

(CONTINUED)

CONTINUED:

                          CHECK-IN AGENT
Here are your boarding passes, and if you'd like to make
your way through security, boarding will begin in just over
an hour.

                          TRUMP
Eric Trump, make sure you have your clear school bag ready
for security to check.

                              The CHECK-IN AGENT moves to push
                              JUNIOR offstage.

                          IVANKA
Daddy, why isn't Jared Kushner coming?

                          TRUMP
Jared Kushner was a great guy, but... Kellyanne Conway, can
you take this one?

                          CONWAY
Sure thing, Mister Trump.
                    (putting her arm around
                     IVANKA)
Ivanka, let me tell you a story about how there are plenty
more fish in the South American Sea.

                              CONWAY and IVANKA exit.

                          ERIC
Hey, where's European mom?

                          TRUMP
She said she's having dinner with a lawyer tonight.

                              Beat, and then HANNITY
                              approaches them.

                          HANNITY
Donald J. Trump.

                              TRUMP turns to him.

                          TRUMP
Sean Hannity.

                                            (CONTINUED)

                          ERIC
Dad, are we going away for a long time? Because Uncle
Mueller promised that he would introduce us all to a
talking snowman.

                          TRUMP
Eric Trump, if you are good and leave us alone, I will buy
you a talking snowman toy from the shop.

                          ERIC
I can be a good boy. If I try hard, I can even be a real
boy.

                     ERIC exits.

                          HANNITY
President Trump, sir.

                          TRUMP
Sean Hannity.

                          HANNITY
Does it have to end this way? I thought that we were all
going to grow old together in prison. You, me, and everyone
else. I thought Betsy DeVos would count her days in prison
in elephants.

                          TRUMP
You could come with us, Sean Hannity. It would be great.

                          HANNITY
But if I leave, who will look after Tucker Carlson? He
needs me as a role model otherwise, he might grow up to be
a respected journalist.

                          TRUMP
You do such fantastic work with that man, Sean Hannity.

                          HANNITY
Will I ever see you again?

                                              (CONTINUED)

CONTINUED:

                              TRUMP
Of course, you will see me again. You will see my face
every day on all of the wanted posters. They are going to
be <u>huge</u>.

                    HANNITY watches as TRUMP exits.

                              HANNITY
You were a good friend, Mister President.

                         A moment, and then HANNITY takes
                         a deep breath as PUTIN enters
                         and places his arm around his
                         shoulders.

                              PUTIN
Don't not worry about Donald. Tell me, how you like to be
world leader in year two thousand and twenty?

                         Together, they exit.

ACT II, SCENE SEVENTEEN | KUSHNER IN THE OVAL OFFICE

                         The OVAL OFFICE, where KUSHNER
                         sits alone behind the desk
                         looking around confused and
                         scared.

                              NARRATOR
                            (entering)
And so we reach at last the end of our first part, and
still yet to show Trump is any sign of a heart. And so
while to South America he now takes flight, there is
another who sits in the Oval Office on this night. For it
is that Jared Kushner, in all the commotion, has received
an unexpected promotion. From the bottom to the top, being
president is now his job. But little is Jared aware of just
how badly he is about to fare.

                         The NARRATOR exits.

                                            (CONTINUED)

>   For a moment, KUSHNER continues
>   to look around, and then
>   suddenly, there's loud banging
>   and lights fill the stage as the
>   ENSEMBLE (as FBI AGENTS) storm
>   on stage and surround him.

                         FBI AGENT #1
We're looking for the President.

>   Beat, and then KUSHNER begins to
>   raise his hands.

                         KUSHNER
I want my mommy.

>   Lights out.

END OF PART ONE

9 781913 408794